STORIES FROM THE

Haunted South

STORIES FROM THE

Haunted South

Alan Brown

University Press of Mississippi   Jackson

www.upress.state.ms.us

The University Press of Mississippi is a member of
the Association of American University Presses.

Copyright © 2004 by University Press of Mississippi
All rights reserved
Manufactured in the United States of America
♾
Library of Congress Cataloging-in-Publication Data

Brown, Alan, 1950 Jan. 12–
    Stories from the haunted South / Alan Brown.
        p. cm.
    Includes bibliographical references (p.) and index.
    ISBN 1-57806-660-3 (cloth: alk. paper)—ISBN 1-57806-661-1
(pbk.: alk. paper)
        1. Ghosts—Southern States. 2. Haunted places—Southern States. I. Title.

BF1472.U6B747   2004
133.1′0975—dc22   2004003485

British Library Cataloging-in-Publication Data available

To my little pumpkins, Andrea and Vanessa

CONTENTS

PREFACE

This book is essentially a sequel to *Haunted Places in the American South*, which was my first attempt to write a volume of ghostlore similar to the works of L. B. Taylor Jr., Nancy Roberts, and Kathryn Tucker Windham. Like *Haunted Places, Stories from the Haunted South* explores the ghostly terrain of Alabama, Arkansas, Florida, Georgia, Kentucky, Louisiana, Mississippi, North Carolina, South Carolina, Tennessee, Texas, and Virginia. Once again, I have combined newspaper accounts of regional hauntings with the oral testimony of witnesses to these events.

The primary difference between *Stories from the Haunted South* and *Haunted Places* is the inclusion of more verbatim comments by people who have actually had experiences in these places or who have heard these stories from a reliable source. Although most of my interviews were conducted over the telephone, I was able to speak to several witnesses face-to-face. Thanks to funding provided by the UWA University Research Grants Committee, I was able to travel to Savannah and New Orleans to collect stories connected with haunted inns, restaurants, and museums. I discovered firsthand what anthropologists and folklorists have been saying for years: that the setting of a storytelling event can have a positive, or a negative, effect on the storyteller's performance. In most cases, the tour guides, concierges, and waitresses seemed to draw inspiration from their surroundings as they painted mental pictures of sightings that had occurred right where we were standing.

A project such as this evolves over a period of time. Before I even started writing the book in 2001, I had at least fifteen places in mind that I wanted to investigate. The names of most of these places came from Dennis William Hauck's indispensable *Haunted Places: The National Directory*. However, my original plan went through several revisions. A few of the places I looked into did not have a well-developed story behind them, like the light that has been seen in a window in Andrew Johnson's birthplace. Sometimes, though, I received tips on haunted places that I had never heard about or read about before. This information was provided by librarians, curators of museums, web sites, and private individuals. Although deviating from my original vision for the book was disconcerting at time, the joy of discovering tales that had not been told outside of their places of origin more than made up for any anxiety I might have encountered along the way.

ACKNOWLEDGMENTS

I am deeply indebted to the following librarians and curators who responded to my request for information: Jim Bagget from the Birmingham Public Library (Birmingham, Alabama); Freddie Deblieux from the Old State Capitol (Baton Rouge, Louisiana); Brenda Dubose from the Anderson College Library (Anderson, South Carolina); Bonnie Hallman from the Huntsville Public Library (Huntsville, Alabama); Linda Hassell from the Whitaker Library at Chowan College (Murfreesboro, North Carolina); Peggy Ledbetter from the DeWitt County Courthouse (Cuero, Texas); Gloria List from the Bodley-Bullock House (Lexington, Kentucky); Elsa Lohman from the Fredericksburg and Spotsylvania National Military Park (Fredericksburg, Virginia); Carol Marcks from the East Baton Rouge Parish Library (Baton Rouge, Louisiana); Linda McDowell from the Butler Center for Arkansas Studies (Little Rock, Arkansas); Lashe Mullins from White Hall State Historic Site (Richmond, Kentucky); and Judy Proffett from the Noxubee County Library (Macon, Mississippi).

I would also like to thank Pamela Decker, Michael Graham, Karen Lundhal, Angela Meredith, Stephanie Routt, Peter Schreiber, Patti Starr, Ken Sumner, Cindy Thuma, David Taylor, Troy Taylor, and Julia Wolf, who served as consultants for this project. Finally, I am grateful to the University of West Alabama (UWA) Research Grants Committee for providing me with funding for this project.

INTRODUCTION

Ghost researcher Troy Taylor defines the term *ghostlore* as "the practice that society has of trying to explain strange events by attaching a legend to them." As substitutes for scientific explanations of spectral lights hovering around swampy areas or odd sounds issuing forth from creaky old houses, ghost stories are woefully inadequate. However, as stimulants for the imagination, ghost tales are much more entertaining than scientific treatises. The highly charged emotions that permeate most ghost legends have thrilled listeners in the Deep South for generations, and they continue to do so in the printed collections of southern ghost stories that have flooded the market in recent years. The stories in this volume are intended to be taken not as irrefutable proof of life after death, but as the regional lore of a people who have lived through generations of war, slavery, illiteracy, and poverty.

Most of the stories in this book are based on historical fact and, therefore, qualify as legends. Whenever possible, I have prefaced each ghost story with a brief biographical sketch of the major places. If the haunted place is some sort of manmade structure, I included a short history of its construction. Presenting the factual side of a story tends to make the more fanciful elements (i.e., the apparition) all the more believable. Only a few of the stories in this book (e.g., "The Lady of the DeWitt County Courthouse Clock") have no basis in fact and are clearly folk tales. This is not to say, though, that visiting the actual setting of a folk tale cannot be as exciting as touring a legendary haunted house. In both cases, the imagination operates to lend the place a ghostly veneer.

Stories from the Haunted South deviates from the standard book of ghost legends in that it includes interviews with several paranormal investigators. Granted, their encounters are, in some cases, less reliable than witnesses who had no prior interest in the supernatural before their sighting. After all, most "ghost hunters" are people who are driven to prove that the spirit can survive the death of the body. My purpose in presenting their findings is not to demonstrate to the reader that ghosts are real. Rather, I believe that their stories represent a relatively new development in oral ghost narratives. The evidence provided by electromagnetic field (EMF) detectors and motion detectors serves the same purpose as names and dates in traditional ghost stories. EMF detectors enable the paranormal investigator to pinpoint disruptions in the magnetic field caused by energy given off by ghosts. It adds a degree of verisimilitude that enhances the suspension of disbelief.

Despite the fact that I am relying on Gutenbergean technology to disseminate my stories, I feel compelled to share with the reader a relatively new source of ghost stories. In the 1990s, electronic media provided a new forum for ghost tales. Television series like the History Channel's *Haunted History* make ghost stories come alive through interviews with eyewitnesses and dramatizations of sightings. The Internet has created the means through which individuals share their encounters in chat rooms and on web sites like "*All about Ghosts.*" I discovered the existence of many of the haunted places in this book on the Internet, and I believe that it can be a viable tool for anyone interested in writing books of ghostlore or for someone who would like to travel to a haunted locale.

As you read through the tales in *Stories from the Haunted South*, you might find yourself asking the question, "Are these stories really true?" When I am asked that question at lectures and readings, I usually answer, "Well, they are true enough to be scary, aren't they?" If the history and legends contained in this volume have prompted you to wonder about the mysteries of death and the hereafter, then I have succeeded in my purpose.

STORIES FROM THE

Haunted South

Alabama

The Alabama Theatre

uring the first half of the century, before the advent of television, millions of Americans sought release from war and the Great Depression at the movies. Each week from the 1910s through the 1940s, Americans went to the "picture show," where they saw movie stars such as Valentino, Helen Hayes, Clark Gable, Carole Lombard, Alan Ladd, Rock Hudson, and Kim Novak. Unlike the cramped multiplexes of today, the theaters back in the "golden age" of motion pictures were justly called palaces. Many of the old-time movie palaces seated from 2,500 to 6,000 patrons at a time. Deluxe palaces boasted first-run features, organs, and stage shows. It is small wonder that studio head Marcus Lowe once remarked, "We sell tickets to theaters, not movies."

Some of the most fanciful and elaborate movie architecture was spawned in the 1920s. One of the South's most elegant movie palaces was Birmingham's Alabama Theatre. It was built in 1927 as a showcase for Paramount films. For fifty-five years, the Alabama Theatre was used primarily to show movies. After the owners of the theater declared bankruptcy in 1987, the building was purchased by Birmingham Landmarks Inc., a nonprofit organization. In 1998, the Alabama Theatre was completely restored to its original 1927 luster. New drapes were installed on the stage, and new carpet was installed in the ladies' lounge. The theater now hosts many live events as well as movies. Over the years, celebrities such as Helen Reddy, Wayne Newton, Lionel Hampton, and Lee Meriwether have performed at the Alabama Theatre. Apparently, the old theater is also home to a music-loving spirit.

Cecil Whitmeyer, the director of the Alabama Theatre, said that there have been several well-documented cases of ghostly encounters in the old theater. One former employee had a very strange experience in the balcony when she first started working in the theater: "She was checking seats for line of sight for a special program that had an interpretation screen above the opera," Whitmeyer said, "and she wanted to make sure that everyone could see. So she was sitting in various seats to check this out. These seats . . . automatically flip up . . . As she sat down in her seat, a seat two seats down went down with her. She immediately got up and left."

Over the years, many people have seen and heard things that could not be explained. "We had a wedding here on Halloween about three years ago," Whitmeyer said, "and the maid of honor said she saw a ghostly image down at the end of the hall of a lady in a red velvet dress. When she walked toward the lady, the image vanished into the wall." People have also reported hearing footsteps and slamming doors. A few have even seen curtains blowing in places where no breeze was present. In 2001, the phenomena attracted the attention of a ghost hunter group, who contacted the Alabama Theatre via the Internet. Although the group did not witness any paranormal events, they did uncover some traces of the supernatural. "They worked with one of our employees here, Janie Hanks, our house manager," said Mr. Whitmeyer. "They found energy up and down where we thought it would be."

One of the strangest incidents at the Alabama Theatre occurred back in 1987. At the time, fund-raiser concerts were being held to assist Birmingham's efforts to save the theater. One Saturday afternoon, five people were practicing in the theater for a benefit concert to be held the next day. Cecil Whitmeyer was playing the organ while a soloist was singing "Memory" from *Cats*. As the soloist was singing a very dramatic part of the song, she caught a glimpse of someone standing behind the stage. Cecil Whitmeyer viewed the apparition as well: "I saw an image walk behind the screen. I thought it was one of the people who were in the theater with me, but all of the people I had with me were out in the auditorium. I didn't know that at the time." Although Mr. Whitmeyer has no idea whom the ghost might be, some have specu-lated that the theater is haunted by the spirit of a long-time musician who played the organ for the movies and shows. Other organists have sensed his presence as well, especially when practicing on Sunday mornings before an afternoon concert.

Although Cecil Whitmeyer and his staff have been startled by the paranormal activity in the building, no one has really felt threatened by the spirits. "Our ghosts must be good ghosts because they haven't caused any real trouble here," Whitmeyer said. In a sense, Mr. Whitmeyer considers the ghost to be his legacy: "Every theater man-ager from 1927 on has passed down to the next theater manager that there is a ghost here. It's almost as if it is part of the job. I was told you will see things, you will hear things, but it's been here forever. It's not a problem. It never causes any difficulty, but there is a ghost here, and you might as well accept it."

The Alabama Theatre is located at 1817 Third Avenue North, Birmingham, Alabama; phone: 205-252-2262.

The Homewood
Public Library

At first glance, the Homewood Public Library bears a close resemblance to a church. Actually, the Homewood Church of Christ owned and used the land and building before the city of Homewood bought the property in 1986. However, before the church was constructed in the 1960s, a vacant farmhouse once stood on the spot. Shortly after the library opened in 1987, the library staff discovered that something still lingers in the building long after closing time.

Assistant library director Deborah Fout claims that she has heard many voices in the library after the lights go out and the doors are closed. Other staff members claim to have heard the voices of women talking and singing emanating from the downstairs area. Roosevelt Hatcher, the information systems manager, first heard the disembodied voices in 1996. While upgrading the computers late one night, Hatcher heard what he thought was a radio: "It sounded like little old ladies chit-chatting and laughing. They were having a good old time." Hatcher began searching the offices in the library to try to find the sources of the voices, but not a single radio appeared to be on. As he walked through the doorway of one of the offices, the voices ceased altogether.

Strange noises, such as the sounds of books falling off the shelves or doors slamming, are also heard when there appears to be no one else around. Library director Edith Harwell had one such experience several years ago: "I was working here late one night. The library was locked up for the night, so there was no one but me in the library. All of a sudden, I heard the sound of car doors slamming. I thought there was somebody in the parking lot, but when I went to the door and looked out, there was nobody there. I was so spooked that I turned off the lights and went home right then and there! I was in such a hurry to leave that I forgot to turn off the alarm. We had to send somebody to the library to turn off the alarm later that night."

Apparently, the paranormal activity within the library escalated between 1996 and 1998 when the library underwent extensive renovation. Strange things started happening from the very beginning of the project. Deborah Fout recalls, "The first day they came in to do their survey work, the project manager came up to me and said, 'What did you-all do? Build your library on top of a graveyard?' I said, 'Why?' And he said because they couldn't get any readings on their instruments. All of their equipment was going crazy out there." Fout had a particularly eerie experience during this time: "When we were in our building project, I stayed here one Friday night. They moved my office downstairs because they were renovating upstairs, and I was in this tiny little office downstairs. There was nobody else in the building, and I was trying to catch up on my work. I always kept my office locked when the library was open. I had to go to the restroom, and there was nobody else in the building, so I just left my door standing open and went to the restroom. Then when I came back, my door was closed. It scared me to death because I thought, 'My keys are in there. I locked my keys in the office, and here I am up here!' And so I checked my door, and it was closed, but it wasn't locked. And I know I left it open. So the next time, when I went to the restroom, I took my keys with me, and I locked the door, and I checked myself on it, and when I came back, the door was open. Then I got my stuff and left."

The most frightening event that took place during the renovations involved a work crew who had been sent to the library to install the sprinkler system between 8:00 P.M. and 4:00 A.M. Deborah Fout recalls this day very well: "This happened one night when they were working on the adult services department. The workmen got so scared they left their tools inside and got the Homewood police department. They said that they had lights going on and off and there were some lightweight metal studs that would move across the floor. There were also electrical cords that danced in the air. The guy who was the head of the group had them all drug tested. One guy refused to work here anymore."

Deborah Fout claims that she and the rest of the staff have taken a philosophical attitude toward the strange occurrences: "We've learned to live with these things. There's nothing you can do about it. And it's not like it's really scary. Nobody's ever seen a ghost." Still, Fout admits that at times, the eerie atmosphere of the library "gets to her": "I used to stay late at night and get caught up on my work, but I don't do it anymore. I used to come in on Sunday mornings too when I didn't go to church and catch up on my work, but I don't do that either. It just got to where I got too spooked. I can't take it anymore."

The Homewood Public Library is located at 1721 Oxmoor Road, Homewood, Alabama; phone: 205-877-8661.

The Julia Tutwiler Learning Resource Center, University of West Alabama

*T*he University of West Alabama has gone through many name changes since it was first established as Livingston Female Academy in 1835. In 1881, President Carlos G. Smith and his assistant, the noted Alabama educator and social reformer Julia Tutwiler, were instrumental in helping the institution achieve status as a normal school. Tutwiler became president in 1890 and served with distinction until she retired as president emeritus in 1910. In the 1950s and 1960s, the increase in enrollment resulted in the construction of a number of new buildings on the campus of the institution now known as Livingston. One of the new buildings was the Julia Tutwiler Library (1960). This modern-looking structure is hardly the place where one would expect to find ghosts. Yet, students and faculty say that the Julia Tutwiler Learning Resource Center is the most haunted building on the campus of the University of West Alabama.

The ghost in the Julia Tutwiler Learning Resource Center first made an appearance on April 11, 1995, when a student named Ray Jordan was studying for a sociology exam in one of the little rooms in the back corner of the first floor. It was getting late, but Ray was not concerned because he believed that the night librarian, Becky Babb, closed up at midnight. At 10:58, Ray was engrossed in his books and notes when he suddenly realized that the lights were going out. He grabbed his books and his backpack, but by the time he reached the circulation desk, he saw Becky Babb walking out the front door. Ray yelled Becky's name, but she did not hear him.

Ray's mounting panic quickly subsided when he noticed the telephone behind the circulation desk. After calling the campus police, Ray sat down behind the desk and began looking over his notes. Soon, he began hearing little sounds: "At first, it wasn't something out of the ordinary. It go so loud that [I began to realize] that they were not just building sounds, but they were sounds of pages being flipped, books being slammed shut, bookshelves being bumped. Those kinds of things. It was really scary because I knew I was the only person in there."

All of a sudden, Ray sensed another presence in the building. He walked into the rear office of the library where he began to feel even more uneasy, as if something were very near to him: "And as I realized that, something just walked right on by me, and that was when my hair almost fell out. And there was a really cool breeze that went by with it, and then it went by again, and then it just kind of settled in a bookshelf there in the office, and I was just in tears." As Ray's fear subsided, he walked out of the office and waited for the campus police to arrive.

A week later, Ray returned to the library, where he noticed the picture of a woman with a familiar face. He asked the librarian about the identity of the woman in the picture, and she said that it was a former professor named Lucille Foust. All at once, everything began to fit together in Ray's mind: "From the very beginning when I felt [its presence], I knew it was a female. And when it walked by me twice, it was like somebody wearing a dress. Whenever a woman walks by in a dress, you feel a little breeze down here, and that's certainly what it felt like."

Lucille Foust was born in Winston-Salem, North Carolina, in 1871. She was a graduate of North Carolina College for Women, and she earned a master's degree at Peabody College, where she taught for a time before coming to Livingston State College. In 1931, she became a professor of education at Livingston State College, a position that she held until her retirement in 1954. Ms. Foust is still remembered by some of the elderly residents of Livingston as the principal of the Laboratory School, which operated on campus in the first half of the twentieth century. Gregor Smith, a retired archivist in the Julia Tutwiler Learning Resource Center, attended grades 1-6 at the Laboratory School in the 1930s. "Back then, it was called the Training Center because that is where student teachers received their training. Ms. Foust was the supervisor, and I remember her as a very intelligent woman. She loved poetry, and I remember having to memorize poems throughout elementary school. It was an excellent school. I did well in everything but math. I'm sure that was my fault. The teachers there were very good, especially Ms. Foust." Ms. Foust retired in 1954 but maintained her keen interest in young people and education until her death on January 1, 1967.

In recent years, several staff members have had encounters with the spirit that most believe is the ghost of Lucille Foust. Nicole Gotschall had two experiences with the ghost in the late 1990s: "The first one happened just after I started working here. I was sitting down at the circulation desk when I heard my name being called just in back of me in the periodical section. When I got up and went to look in the periodical section, there was nobody there. The second time, it was a Saturday. I was here all by myself. There was not a soul in the library at all. Then at three o'clock in the afternoon, I heard two books fall to the floor upstairs. I was downstairs in the circulation desk. Then I heard someone running from one side of the library to the other."

Longtime night librarian Becky Babb has observed more ghostly activity in the library than anyone else. Although she has worked at the library for sixteen years, she began noticing the ghostly activity in the mid-1990s. Becky says that for over five years, strange noises have been commonplace in the library at night. A good example is a frightening experience she had one dark, cold February night in 2003: "I was sitting at the front desk at ten o'clock, and all of a sudden, I heard three of the cabinet doors back in the office slam shut. It was like three big bumps. I jumped out of my chair and went and looked, but there was nobody there. There was one boy back in the computer lab, but other than that, I was by myself. If that boy hadn't been in the library, I would have left. I've heard stuff back there before, but not that loud. Several times, I've heard books fall off the shelves down here, but when I walk over to investigate, there's nothing on the floor. Sometimes, I hear noises upstairs when there's nobody up there, like the sound of chairs being pushed out from behind a desk. I used to hear the bathroom doors open."

Becky has even gotten "up close and personal" with the library's ghost: "One night a couple of weeks ago, I felt really weird here all by myself. I could just feel something standing over me. This wasn't as bad as what happened to me a couple of years ago. I was sitting out at the front desk, and I could feel something run across my back and down my arm. It really felt like fingers. This is the only time I ever felt it."

In February 2003, Becky had a very strange encounter with an antique wheelchair that is kept in a conference room on the second floor: "When I went upstairs, that wheelchair was sitting at the top of the stairs. It was facing me like it was fixing to roll down. If a puff of wind had blown behind it, it would have been gone! I thought, 'Kids had to have done this,' but there wasn't a soul up there. I left the chair there. I wasn't about to roll it back into the conference room. I don't know how it got back in there."

According to Becky, one of the campus policemen had a terrifying experience in the library several years ago: "Years ago, the campus police used to come inside the library at about two or three A.M. and read the newspapers. One night, one of the policemen was sitting in one of the chairs out front by the main desk reading when he looked up at the glass doors and saw the reflection of something floating behind him. He ran out the doors and has not been back since. I even called him one night to come over, and he wouldn't show up."

Dr. Neil Snider, the director of the Julia Tutwiler Learning Resource Center, has a theory as to why Ms. Foust's ghost haunts the library, even though she did not work there: "After Ms. Foust died, Fannie Pickens Ingliss was commissioned to do a portrait of her. The portrait was to hang in Foust Hall. When they made the plaque, they listed her as 'Principle of the Laboratory School.' People who knew Ms. Foust were horrified because she couldn't tolerate misspelled words. So they removed the portrait from Foust Hall, which is named for her, and placed it in a closet. In the 1980s, the portrait was discovered when the closets in Foust Hall were cleaned out. Gregor Smith and I decided to hang the portrait in the Alabama Room [the archives]. We tried many, many times to remove the plaque, but it had been put on there with epoxy glue or some other kind of substance, and we could not remove it. We never thought to have it reframed. After Nikki and others started talking about seeing shadows and feeling something, I had an occasion to go to the Alabama Room, and I looked, and the plaque was gone. So how did it get removed from the portrait? I think Ms. Foust did it because she couldn't stand the misspelled words."

Dr. Snider's second theory regarding the presence in the library explains why the sightings began in 1995: "When Dr. Lyon came here in 1947, the unmarried women faculty, including the unmarried women teachers at the lab school, lived on the second floor of Webb Hall, which was the girls' dormitory at the time. Ms. Foust was among the professors who lived there. It has been alleged that Dr. Lyon made a public statement that the first thing he had to do as academic dean was to get the old maids out of Webb. His statement made the ladies furious, and they all moved out, except Ms. Foust. She refused to give up her room, even after she retired. She was living in Webb Hall when she died. People who knew her said she never got over Dr. Lyon's alleged remark. I wonder if Ms. Foust carried her resentment about being called publicly an old maid to her grave and now haunts the library because Dr. Lyon's portrait has been hanging in the library since 1995. The description some people have given about the library ghost fits the physical description of Ms. Foust, a tall slender woman."

While it is true that several librarians and staff members have had what they believe to have been brushes with the supernatural in the Julia Tutwiler Learning Resource Center, not everyone believes the library is haunted. Former archivist Gregor Smith has serious doubts that the ghost—if it really is a ghost—is the spirit of Lucille Foust: "Ms. Foust was a very serious-minded woman. I'm sure she didn't believe in ghosts, and I doubt that she would have turned into one." Most of those who do believe in the library's ghost, however, are not about to let a little haunting keep them from doing their jobs. Becky Babb, like so many other staff members, has learned to live with the ghost: "I guess I've gotten used to the noises. It helps that I only work from ten o'clock to eleven o'clock every night, so I'm not here long enough for something really bad to happen. When I get really scared, I tell the ghost, 'I'm only going to stay in the library a few minutes longer. Then you can have the place!'"

Livingston is on the extreme western border of Alabama, about six miles east of Interstate 20/59; phone: 800-621-8044. Take Exit 17 off Highway I20/59. Turn north and drive two miles to Highway 11. Turn right and drive two more miles. The Julia Tutwiler Learning Resource Center is on the corner of Highway 11 and Bibb Graves Drive.

Radio Station WZPQ

Radio stations in Alabama and Mississippi have the built-in potential of becoming haunted, not because they perpetuate the voices of dead singers like Buddy Holly and John Lennon, but because so many small stations occupy buildings that were once private residences. One such radio station is WZPQ in Jasper, Alabama. The station is located in an old house that was once owned by George Vines, a Mercury dealer in Jasper during the 1950s. When the station moved to the old Vines house in 1975, it was WWWB, but it changed its call letters in the 1980s to WZPQ. According to the personnel at the station, George Vines has never really left.

The best source for ghost stories centering around WZPQ is Pamela Decker, who worked as a disc jockey there in 1992. At the time, Decker was studying broadcast journalism at Walker College. "I was really lucky that I'd gotten a job doing what I was studying for my major," Decker said. "I was on top of the world, but I knew that there had to be a catch." The catch turned out to be a ghost. For two and a half years, she experienced phenomena that can best be described as otherworldly.

Decker soon traced the source of the haunting back to George Vines: "I became acquainted with people from other radio stations who had gotten their start there back in the 1970s when the station first moved into this building. They told me that this house had belonged to a man named George. He was an actual person. He died back in the days when they brought the body home to lie in state in the parlor or the living room." George's body lay in the bay window area where the control panel is located now. For over a quarter of a century, radio personnel reported strange occurrences at this spot. However, Decker maintains that George's ghost makes his presence known throughout the radio station.

Pamela Decker first realized that something about the radio station "wasn't quite right" when she started working in the south office. She was particularly annoyed by some of the strange disturbances that occurred while she was on the air: "Many times when I worked evenings, late nights, and on weekends, alone, I would hear the back door open and shut, and blinds on the back door rattle against the plate glass. The doorknob rattled too." Pamela added that if she tried to ignore George's antics, she would see that ghostly figure walk by the control room door: "It started out with a shadow passing by the door. I only saw it out of the corner of my eye, but it appeared to be about five feet, six inches or five feet, seven inches tall. I could make out that he looked to be dressed in a red jacket. He'd swing his arms as if he was walking in a swift gait back and forth down the hall and back up the hall. And it didn't stop until I'd turn my head and look up and down the hallway and acknowledge his presence. He seemed to be a playful spirit. He just wanted to be noticed. That's what I concluded after a while."

Other noises made it particularly difficult for her to concentrate when she was all by herself. For example, sometimes at two or three o'clock in the morning, the production studio door opened and shut by itself. On several occasions, the restroom toilet flushed by itself. "I'd even hear the lid lift up," Pamela said, "which is why I am pretty sure the ghost is a male."

Like many spirits, George enjoys playing with light switches. "Upon leaving for the night," Pamela said, "we had a checklist of things to turn off before we left. We had to turn off all the lights in the station except for a fluorescent light in the kitchen. Many times, while I was pulling out of the parking lot, I would look back, and the lights would still be on."

Pamela's most unnerving experiences at the station happened shortly after she was hired. "My sister drove by on Ninth Avenue and saw through the control room window that a man was standing behind me one evening when I was working on the air, but that was not possible because I was there alone. At that point in my employment there, I had not shared with any of my friends or family that I was working in a haunted radio station. When she told me this about five months after it occurred, my blood ran cold!"

According to stories told to Decker, some employees have had even more personal encounters with George than she did. "Others experienced hearing their names being called from other rooms or offices, and one lady even had her hair stroked when she was in the control room." Still, most of the employees at the radio station learned to take the weird occurrences in stride. "Other employees who worked there before I did and after I left experienced the same things I did," Decker said. "We all brushed it off as our imagination, but after a while, we knew it couldn't just be imagination." Most people living with ghosts come to realize that the ghosts who live with them won't hurt them, and they also come to accept the visitors as long term. The employees at radio WZPQ have accepted George and believe that he is staying for good. Pamela said, "The experiences are sort of enjoyable, and it is fascinating to work in a haunted radio station."

Radio Station WZPQ is at 409 Ninth Avenue, Jasper, Alabama; phone: 205-384-3461.

Huntsville Depot

In the public mind, Huntsville, Alabama, is a city of the future, thanks in large part to the George C. Marshall Space Flight Center, which was established here in 1960, and to work done by Werner von Braun. However, Huntsville is also a city with a glorious past, preserved in its historic buildings, like the Huntsville Depot. Long before Huntsville became associated with space travel, it was an important link on the Memphis and Charleston Railroad Company. In 1850, it was decided that the rail route would definitely go through Huntsville. On October 13, 1855, the General Garth puffed its way into Huntsville for the first time and stopped at a small frame building. In 1857, an engine house and machine shop were built. The passenger shed and the ticket office were completed in 1858, and a car shop was finished two years later. In 1860, the three-story brick depot on Church Street was completed. It housed the Memphis and Charleston Railroad Company Eastern Division Headquarters in several plush offices on the second floor. The first floor had separate waiting rooms for men and women, a baggage room, and a ticket office. Bunk rooms were provided for train crews on the third floor. The Huntsville Depot remained as originally constructed until 1912 when the Southern Railway remodeled the interior first floor. The depot served as the transportation focal point for the community until the late 1960s when the Southern Railway discontinued passenger service through Huntsville. On September 10, 1971, the depot building was listed on the National Register of Historic Places. A month later, it was purchased by the city of Huntsville. It now stands as a relic of a bygone era, a brick-and-mortar ghost from the era of the Iron Horse. Some say that ghosts from the depot's Civil War past still inhabit the old depot.

The Huntsville Depot played a very important role in Alabama's Civil War history. When General O. M. Mitchell captured Huntsville on April 11, 1862, his primary objective was the depot and the telegraph office located inside. Later in the day, Mitchell wired his superiors, "We have captured about 200 prisoners, 15 locomotives, a large number of passenger, box and platform cars, the telegraphic apparatus and offices, and two southern mails. We have at length succeeded in cutting the great artery of railway intercommunication between the Southern states." Mitchell's soldiers captured practically all the engines and railroad cars of the Memphis and Charleston Railroad, which were taken to Huntsville pending removal to a more secure place.

The two hundred Confederate soldiers captured by Mitchell's army had, ironically, been sent to Huntsville to rest and recover from the Battle of Shiloh. Some of them were on furlough, but a large number had been wounded. They were held at the Huntsville Depot for ten days before being transported to a northern prison. During their internment at the prison, the ladies of Huntsville gave the men food and water and provided medical attention. One of these ladies was Mrs. William D. Chadwick. In her diary, she wrote that none of the prisoners took the loyalty oath to the Union. She also mentioned that two Confederate prisoners escaped by putting on Yankee uniforms and walking out the front door of the depot. Except for an eleven-month period, the Federals occupied Huntsville for the remainder of the war.

The depot continued to serve the citizens of Huntsville until the late 1960s. It is now the nucleus of the Museum of Transportation. When the station was being renovated in the 1980s, workers on the third floor sanded away paint applied on the walls in the early 1900s and discovered writing under the paint. Most of this graffiti had been written by Union and Confederate soldiers during the Civil War. It covers the walls so thickly that one message or name often overlaps another. Some of the writing is quite poignant. For example, one of the signatures was penciled into the plaster in 1864 by a Union soldier named Harris Grover. Then a few months later, a friend of his wrote Grover's epitaph under his name: "Harris Grover, Co. K 12th Illinois, was killed in battle 22nd July 1864. He lived in Laporte, Indiana. His name shall be remembered by true patriots." A glass cover has been placed over the graffiti to protect it.

Bonnie Hallman, a librarian at the Huntsville Public Library and a Civil War reenactor, is convinced that the Huntsville Depot is haunted. She first suspected that there was something strange about the depot when she attended meetings there on the third floor: "We used to go up a modern elevator to the third floor for meetings. I like going up the stairs because they are so beautiful. It was always fun going up the stairs, but coming down the stairs was a different proposition because on the second-floor landing was an icy spot that I would get caught in some times. Other people experienced it too, but not everyone. I didn't get these feelings every time myself, but I am sure that there is a cold spot there. I have gotten the impression of a Union soldier standing guard there. It was definitely hostile. Sometimes when I experienced the cold spot, I would ask myself, 'Do I run through the cold spot down the stairs or run through the cold spot up the stairs?' This was not an easy decision to make."

Bonnie admits that the "cold" feeling she gets on the stairs sometimes is difficult to validate. However, she shared another ghostly experience outside the depot with several witnesses: "We had a lot of functions at the depot. We put on a Civil War Days program at the depot at least one weekend a year. We had a camp out there on the grounds and actually spent the night out there. The spectators would come the next day. Friday night was just for us. There were a number of us who had just arrived and set up camp, and we went over to the courtyard because it's paved and it's a more comfortable place to sit around. After a while, I looked up at the third-floor window, and I saw what looked like a light up there. Of course, the depot was closed, and everything was dark. And so I said to the others, 'Look, is someone up there? Did they leave a light on?' But then the light began growing stronger. Suddenly, there was a figure standing in the window holding the light. We stood there and watched him absolutely amazed. It was early in the evening, and nobody had been drinking. There were probably seven or eight of us watching the ghost. The light he was holding was bright enough to illuminate his form. It was a Confederate soldier. He wore a jacket but not a hat. His face was indistinct, but as he turned toward us, it seemed as though he could see us. We stood there looking at each other for the longest time. We were just fascinated. He was probably in the window for at least ten minutes. Then the image faded, and the light went out."

Even though Bonnie and the other reenactors had just had a paranormal experience, they were not really terrified by what they saw. "The ghost did not appear to be threatening," Bonnie said. "I think it was because he realized that we were southerners as well."

The Huntsville Depot can be found at 320 Church Street, Huntsville, Alabama; phone: 800-678-1819.

Arkansas

Henderson State University

Arkadelphia is in many ways the quintessential American small town. Situated within the foothills of the Ouachita Mountains in southwestern Arkansas, Arkadelphia is home to a population of ten thousand people. Like many small towns in the United States, Arkadelphia's livelihood is closely linked with that of higher education. Unlike most towns of its size, though, Arkadelphia has two small colleges, Henderson State University and Ouachita Baptist University. For many years, these two institutions were arch rivals, due in large part to their differences in values and religion. Henderson State University and Ouachita Baptist University are linked, however, by a tragedy that occurred over eighty years ago.

The legend of the ghost of Henderson State University is set in the 1920s when a young man named Joshua fell in love with Jane, a girl from neighboring Ouachita Baptist University. Although they were deeply devoted to each other, their romance suffered from the objections of their friends, many of whom accused the two lovers of "consorting with the enemy." Mary Jo Mann, a Henderson graduate and local historian, says that Joshua's friends probably gave him such a hard time not just because Jane was so religious and introverted, but also because she attended a school that was far different from Henderson: "Going to Ouachita in those days meant no parties and hardly any dating. They really never had a chance because no one from Henderson would ever think about seeing someone from Ouachita in those days," Mann said, "and if they did, they could expect to feel the heat from their friends." Pushed almost to the breaking point, Joshua decided to break up with his girlfriend.

Down through the years, the story has acquired two different endings. According to one version, Joshua started dating a girl from his own university. When Jane discovered that Joshua was taking his new girlfriend to the homecoming dance, she committed suicide. In the second ending to the story, Joshua ended their relationship just before the homecoming dance. Heartbroken, she decided that life without Joshua was not worth living. She returned to her dorm room and put on a black dress and veil, suitable attire for her mournful mood. She then walked over to the edge of one of the cliffs lining the Ouachita River and plunged to her death. Every year at homecoming, Jane's melancholy spirit returns to Henderson, searching for the ones who made Joshua break up with her.

This old ghost story is still very much "alive," in a manner of speaking, on Henderson's campus. Mary Jo Mann tells the story of "The Lady in Black" every fall during her welcome speech to incoming freshmen. "It really does give me chill bumps when someone mentions her," Mann said. "There isn't a person on the Henderson campus [who] doesn't know something about the story." Angela Welch, a junior at Henderson, feels the same way about the story: "When I first heard the story, it gave me goose bumps. The way she [Mann] tells the story made me believe that the ghost was real." Angela began to suspect that the story of the Lady in Black was more than just an old legend in 2000 when she and a group of friends were walking back to the girls' dorm around midnight on homecoming weekend. All at once, Angela saw a faint figure dressed in black leaving one of the buildings on campus: "I couldn't tell what it was at first. Then someone screamed out that it was the Lady in Black," Welch said. "I just screamed and ran into my dorm room. I really believe it was her because you could see a veil of all black and there was a kind of glow around her body."

Thanks to Mary Jo Mann, the popularity of the legend has attracted the attention of the local media. Many news organizations throughout the state have covered the story of the Lady in Black. The most widely known report was broadcast in the 1980s by Chuck Dovish, from KTHV Channel 11 in Little Rock, for his weekly special "Traveling Arkansas." "With Mary Jo Mann's help, we were able to go out to the cliff where she [Jane] supposedly jumped," Dovish said. "It was really an odd feeling to be there because the cliff was so steep and you could almost feel her presence. We did a short reenactment for the show and had to get special permission from Ouachita to even get out there to the site." Since Dovish's broadcast, the cliff where Jane is believed to have jumped has been sealed off by Ouachita Baptist University, which owns the cliff. Now no one is permitted to visit the site without a university escort.

Sightings of the Lady in Black have been rare, mainly because she only appears once a year at homecoming. Like many students at Henderson State University, Mary Jo Mann graduated before she had an opportunity to see the ghost. Still, she has not given up hope: "I have never had the chance to see her myself. But I feel like I will have my chance one day."

Arkadelphia is seventy miles southwest of Little Rock on Interstate 30. The address for Henderson State University is 1100 Henderson Street, Arkadelphia, AR 71929; phone: 501-246-5511.

Hornibrook Mansion
(The Empress of Little Rock)

*H*ornibrook Mansion stands as a mute testament to the genteel lifestyle enjoyed by the wealthiest residents of Little Rock, Arkansas, in the Victorian Era. Designed by Casper Kusener and Max Orlopp, Hornibrook Mansion was finally completed in 1888 after six years of construction. Building costs amounted to $20,000, a royal sum when compared to the $2,500–$3,500 required to build an average house at that time. Building materials used in the construction of Hornibrook Mansion included brick, stucco, wood, rock, crystal, limestone, and granite. Wood from six native trees was used in the floors. Every known convenience was built into the lavish nineteenth-century home, including an intercom system, three "indoor" water closets, running hot water, steam heat, and electricity. Apparently, it comes with its own ghost as well.

After the Civil War, James Hornibrook moved from Toronto to Little Rock. He set himself up as a saloon-keeper, a profession that still bore the stigma of having been banned during the occupation of the Civil War. With the experience and backing of his merchant family, Hornibrook soon became one of the richest men in Arkansas. Despite his immense wealth, Hornibrook and his family were not admitted into the "polite society" of Little Rock. Angered by the fact that his competitor, Angelo Marre, was allowed to build a fine home on fashionable Scott Street, Hornibrook built his ostentatious manor as a means of flaunting his wealth in the faces of those who had rejected him socially. He also held poker games in the tower and hired boys to serve as lookouts for the authorities. Unfortunately, Hornibrook did not live in his beautiful home for long. He died of an apoplectic stroke at the front gate at the age of forty-nine.

Over the next one hundred years, the house underwent a series of incarnations. Hornibrook's wife, Margaret, lived in the house until her death in 1893. The Hornibrooks' eldest daughter, Lessie Peay, and her husband moved in to help care for the younger Hornibrook children. In 1897, the house was leased to the Arkansas Women's College. Insurance agent and former federal marshal Asbury S. Fowler purchased the mansion around the turn of the century. After he died in 1922, his widow continued to live there until financial collapse during the Great Depression forced her to move into a smaller house. The house remained vacant until the early 1940s when it became a women's boardinghouse. In 1947, the mansion was converted into a nursing home. In the 1970s, it became a private residence once again but was eventually broken up into apartments. A halfway house was also set up there in the 1980s. Then in December 1993, Robert Blair and Sharon Welch Blair bought it and turned the old house formerly known as Hornibrook Mansion into a luxurious bed and breakfast renamed "The Empress of Little Rock."

Since the Blairs opened their bed and breakfast in 1994, they have received numerous reports from their guests of strange occurrences in the old building. Although Sharon has never seen anything out of the ordinary in the mansion, her husband has.

One day while the house was being renovated, Robert Blair was upstairs redoing a room when he saw a man dressed in 1800s clothing descending the stairs. The figure was wearing a black Homburg hat. Because there was no one else there, Robert was bewildered by the man's sudden appearance. His first thought was, "What is he doing here?" After a few seconds, the man vanished. Over the years, guests have written letters to the Blairs describing similar experiences in the old mansion.

On October 31, 2002, the Central Arkansas Society for Paranormal Research (CASPR) conducted a scientific investigation of Hornibrook Mansion. CASPR was founded in 2001 by Karen Lundhal and Trish McCuen.

Lundahl's EMF detectors provided the group with some fascinating readings: "We had a really remarkable experience with the EMF detectors. I was very pleased with it. I was doing an interview with Channel 7 news, which is our major station here in Arkansas, and in the tower room, which is the place where Mr. Hornibrook would hang out and play poker and drink. He could look out the window and see his saloon down the street to watch the competition and to see if he was about to be raided by the cops. He still hangs out there now. We had gone into the tower room previously and swept it to see if we were getting any readings, and there was nothing in there electrical or otherwise that could have set off the detectors accidentally. Suddenly, the reporter who was with us said, 'Did you feel that?' She said she felt cold for some reason. The tower is a big, round area, and we were all standing with our backs in a circle. Trish [McCuen] had the EMF detector. She held it toward Mary [the reporter], and it made a whining sound. Mary said, 'Oh, my gosh!' and she was standing there shivering. And then someone across the room said, 'Oh my gosh, it's cold over here.' Trish walked from Mary over to the person who was feeling the cold spot, and when she was between ten and twelve inches from that person, the EMF detector started going off."

Within a few seconds, the entity began to move around the room. The group followed it with their EMF detector into the attic just off from the tower room. The Channel 7 cameras captured the entire "ghost hunt" on film: "During the Channel 7 interview, there was a lot of action going on in a corner of the attic, so I told the reporter, 'Come on over here. You've got to see this!' So part of the interview on Channel 7 showed what was happening with that EMF detector in the attic. It showed one of our investigators saying, 'It's right here! It's right here!' And the EMF detector was going crazy. There was nothing physical there. The investigator also had something grab him on the back of the neck. Then he moved away. All of a sudden, the EMF detector stopped. I went back to the same spot and held the EMF detector over it to see if maybe there was something electrical there. I held it toward the floor, I held it to the ceiling, I held it to the rafters. There was nothing! It was definitely a paranormal experience. It had to be a very powerful entity to set the EMF detector off like that. I have never had readings like that in other places I have investigated."

Hornibrook Mansion stands as proof that some owners invest their home with their personality. James Hornibrook was a stubborn, contentious man who refused to change his ways simply because he lived in one of Little Rock's elite neighborhoods. He was very attached to his elegant mansion when he was alive and apparently still is.

The Empress of Little Rock is located at 2120 South Louisiana Street, Quapaw Quarter Historic District, Little Rock, Arkansas; phone: 501-371-7966.

Old State House

esigned by Gideon Shryock, the Old State House in Little Rock is the oldest surviving state capitol west of the Mississippi River. The construction of this magnificent Greek Revival structure was begun in 1833 and completed in 1842. The building served as the capitol when Arkansas became a state in 1836. It contains two chambers once used by the state legislature and the supreme court. Now a museum, the renovated building houses a multimedia display of Arkansas history and nationally recognized collections of Arkansas art, pottery, Civil War battle flags, African American quilts, and the inaugural gowns of governors' wives. The Old State House was catapulted into the spotlight in 1992 and 1996 when it became the scene of President William Jefferson Clinton's election night celebrations. However, the historic building is also memorialized in a ghost story that has received national attention. Ironically, the origin of the tale is as fascinating as the legend itself.

History records that a fight broke out during Arkansas's very first legislative session in December 1837. The Speaker of the House, Colonel John Wilson, had gotten into a heated argument with Major J. J. Anthony, the representative from Randolph County, over who should handle the payment of bounties for the killing of timber wolves. Anthony sarcastically asserted the bounties should be handled not by a magistrate, but by the president of the Real Estate Bank. Wilson, who was the president of the Real Estate Bank, took this remark as an insult. Drawing his nine-inch Bowie knife, Wilson jumped from the stage and lunged toward Anthony, who retaliated by drawing his own twelve-inch Bowie knife. Despite being stabbed in his guard arm, Wilson brought his knife up into Anthony's chest and killed him. The entire fight lasted twenty seconds. Later, Wilson was acquitted on the grounds of "excusable homicide," but he lost his seat in the assembly. Traditionally, John Wilson has been identified as the apparition that has been sighted wandering the corridors of the Old State House. He is usually described as a sad ghost wearing a frock coat.

Not everyone is convinced that the ghost is the spirit of John Wilson, though. Some speculate that the specter might be the ghost of another unfortunate politician. In 1872, Elisha Baxter was declared governor in a disputed election. Believing that he had been cheated, his opponent, Joseph Brooks, staged a coup of the house seventeen months later. To prevent Baxter from attempting to reclaim the office, Brooks moved a cannon to the State House lawn. Still convinced that he was the rightful governor, Baxter set up an another office down the street. The dispute was settled only after President Grant became involved. Baxter was declared the legitimate governor, and Brooks was forced to retire. Some staff members believe that Brooks's spirit haunts the Old State House because he is still upset about being ousted from the governor's office.

As fantastic as the incidents involving John Wilson and Elisha Baxter sound, they are a genuine part of Arkansas history. The ghost story connected with the Old State House, on the other hand, might not be. Longtime employee Larry Ahart is skeptical: "We looked into it [the ghost story] and determined that it was concocted about 1950. It doesn't exist prior to that. There was an article in the *Arkansas Democrat*, which is a local newspaper. The writer used an elaborate conceit where a woman slipped into the building at night and met the ghost of the architect and talked to him about the building. What happened was that it had a spooky picture of the building and the headline, 'Do Ghosts Walk the Halls?' And after that, there was this ghost story. Apparently, there's no record of anything we can find before that. It was concocted out of whole cloth to promote the building. There are a lot of legends like that that are PR. For some reason, people with old houses have to have a ghost, or it's not really interesting. Mrs. Lore, who was the first curator of the museum, led the coalition of ladies that saved the building.

She hated the ghost story and fought against it. She finally broke a hip, and another woman replaced her, and the first thing she did was bring in a team of mediums. They had a séance and went stalking the ghost through the halls. The way the story works here is that it started as the ghost of the architect, but that doesn't make any sense because he never even came here, so they made it the ghost of J. J. Anthony, a representative who was killed in a knife fight in the House of Representatives in 1837. It's supposed to be his ghost."

In his twenty years at the Old State House, Larry Ahart has never seen a ghost, but others have. "We had a woman who worked here who said she saw it," Ahart said, "but I think that's the power of suggestion. The place is kind of creepy. It kind of moans and groans at night." Even though Ahart and the other employees do not include the ghost story as part of the tour, it appears that the old tale has become as much a part of the Old State House as the nineteenth-century furnishings. "There's a scrapbook here with that article in it," Ahart said, "and Mrs. Lore wrote in the margin that she cursed the day that that article was written because she can't get rid of the ghost and she's afraid it scares the children who come to the museum."

The Old State House Museum is located at 300 West Markham Street, Little Rock, Arkansas; phone: 501-371-1749.

Booneville Tuberculosis Sanitarium

*T*he Booneville Tuberculosis Sanitarium was created on May 31, 1909, by the Arkansas legislature, which acquired 973 acres of land four miles from Booneville. In 1911, the legislature appropriated $60,000 for support of the institution. The first patients were not admitted until 1918, probably because it took a long time to get the sanitarium operational. It ceased functioning as a tuberculosis sanitarium between 1974 and 1975 when doctors began treating tuberculosis patients in hospitals instead of institutionalizing them. Today, the first floor of the old building houses the Human Growth Center. The basement where the morgue was located and the upper floors have been abandoned and are slowly deteriorating. The tuberculosis center would have probably been forgotten altogether were it not for the stories locals told about encountering ghosts there late at night. Only one paranormal group—the Central Arkansas Society for Paranormal Research—has been given permission to investigate the tuberculosis center. According to Karen Lundahl, a member of CASPR, their visit to the old building garnered some very convincing evidence of life after death.

Karen and her group visited the Booneville Tuberculosis Center in October 2002. Here, she had some of the most extraordinary experiences she has ever had on a ghost hunt: "The first time we were there, we were sitting at the end of the fifth-floor hall—three other people and I. We were staring down the corridor into the darkness to see what we could see. It was very quiet. No noise, no light, no nothing. Suddenly, a green glowing light started coming right at me like a train would, straight in my face. As it got close to us, it swerved and went into the wall. That was very unsettling. It was like, 'Wow!'"

Each person in the group had strange experiences on this particular visit. Karen Lundahl recalls, "My husband heard water running in the basin, and he said, 'Can you hear that?' I said, 'What?' He said, 'I can hear water running.' He heard it distinctly, and there's no running water in there. We were right outside a hospital room that had a sink, but there was no water. And the other guy heard soft singing, and he said, 'Can you hear those people singing?' Two of us saw the green glowing light. At least I had someone to back me up on that one. The other girl who was up there claimed to have seen an apparition walking down the hall and turning around." The fact that not all of these experiences could be corroborated by other members of the group does not diminish Lundahl's belief that they were witnesses to paranormal events.

The investigation also yielded some phenomenal video footage of orbs, streaking balls of light that some people believe contain spiritual energy: "There's one ball of light that comes from in back of a door at the end of the fourth-floor hallway where we had the most activity on videotape. If you blow it up full-screen on your computer, you can see that it originated from behind a glass door. It came from around the side of the door, and it almost looks startled. Then it comes around through the door and comes down the hallway and lights up very brightly. We could almost see the thought processes there. It perceived itself needing to go through the doorway. I've seen orbs go through objects before." The almost calculated movement of the orbs on the videotape supports Lundahl's opinion that orbs do not perceive the world as we see it. "They may not be aware that they are dead," Lundahl says. "They may actually see the corridor of the hospital the way it looked in 1940 when they died of tuberculosis." The CASPR group also took still photographs of the same areas that were videotaped. Several of the images captured in the photographs correspond to what showed up on the videotape.

The members even encountered a polite ghost in the Booneville Tuberculosis Sanitarium. Midway through their investigation, they decided to review the videotape they had just shot. Karen said that they were sitting around watching the orbs fly around them on the videotape inside the sanitarium when her sister said, "You're so beautiful. Thank you! Thank you!" Almost immediately, a deep, soft voice responded, "You're so welcome!"

Lundahl believes that the Booneville Tuberculosis Sanitarium has become a hotbed of paranormal activity because of the thousands of people who suffered and died there: "Before antibiotics, tuberculosis was a terrible disease. It was very traumatic to be sent there. You were separated from your family. You were lonely." The research Lundahl conducted prior to her visit to the sanitarium revealed that during one year, eight people committed suicide there.

Unfortunately, CASPR's investigation of the Booneville Tuberculosis Sanitarium will probably be the last. "It's falling apart and filled with asbestos, so the state will no longer let us in there," Lundahl said. "They won't let anyone in the building. We wore masks the last time we were in there." Even though the group's trip to the old building yielded some fascinating images and sounds, Lundahl is not entirely disappointed that she will not be allowed to return: "The place is a health hazard, and I don't know if it's really worth it. The group is exploring the possibility of putting a 'ghost cam' there so we can actually monitor the four floors."

Florida

Henry Morrison Flagler Museum

A merican culture as we know it was born between 1865 and 1929. Christened the "Gilded Age" by Mark Twain, it was a period of remarkable technological growth. Many of the inventions that have become part of the fabric of the daily lives of Americans, such as the telephone and the light bulb, came into being at this time. The World's Columbian Exposition, held in Chicago, highlighted the achievements of this gaudy, marvelous age. The captains of industry who steered America into the modern age became incredibly wealthy. Many of these magnates, like J. P. Morgan and Andrew Carnegie, built luxurious mansions that became show-places for their wealth. One of the most sumptuous of these estates, Whitehall, is also one of the most haunted.

Henry Morrison Flagler, the builder of Whitehall, was born on January 2, 1830, in Hopewell, New York. When he was fourteen years old, he moved to Bellevue, Ohio, where he got a job in a grain store at a salary of five dollars per month and room and board. Five years later, he was promoted to the sales staff. In 1852, Flagler and his half-brother, Dan Harkness, became partners in D. M. Harkness and Company. Flagler married Mary Harkness in 1853. They became the parents of three children, Jennie Louise, Carrie, and Harry Harkness Flagler. In 1862, Henry and his brother-in-law, Barney York, founded the Flagler and York Salt Company. However, the demand for salt dropped dramatically after the Civil War, and Flagler lost fifty thousand dollars. His fortunes improved considerably, however, in 1867 when John D. Rockefeller made Flagler a partner in his burgeoning oil company. On January 10, 1870, their joint venture became the Standard Oil Company. Flagler's happiness was tarnished by his wife's escalating health problems. After visiting Jacksonville, Florida, for the winter, Mary died on May 1881. Two years later, Flagler married his wife's nurse, Ida Alice Shourds.

After traveling with his new wife to St. Augustine, Florida, Flagler found the city's hotels to be woefully inadequate. Realizing Florida's potential as a mecca for tourists, Henry decided to explore the state's business potential. While remaining on the board of directors of Standard Oil, Flagler built the 540-room Ponce de Leon Hotel in 1885. In order to provide transportation for the guests at his luxury hotel, Flagler purchased the Jacksonville, St. Augustine and Halifax Railroad. In 1894, Flagler completed the 1,150-room Royal Poinciana Hotel in Palm Beach. Two years later, Flagler built the Palm Beach Inn. To convince Flagler to extend the railroad to what is now Miami, the Florida East Coast Canal and Transportation, the Boston and Florida Atlantic Coast Land Company, and private landowners offered him free land. In 1896, Flagler built streets and instituted the first water and power system in the city that he christened "Miami." One year later, Flagler opened the exclusive Royal Palm Hotel in Miami.

On August 24, 1901, Flagler married his third wife, a beautiful southern girl thirty-seven years his junior named Mary Lily Kenan. He was still married to his second wife, Ida, who had been institutionalized for mental illness since 1895. However, the Florida legislature paved the way for his marriage by passing a bill making incurable insanity grounds for divorce. In 1902, Flagler built Whitehall Mansion as a wedding present for his new wife. The palatial mansion, which was to become the Flaglers' winter home, was constructed by the New York firm of McKim, Mead, and White, the same firm that had collaborated on the design for the New York Public Library and the Fifth Avenue mansion of Henry Clay Frick. On March 30, 1902, the *New York Herald* described Flagler's 55-room, 60,000-square-foot home as "More wonderful than any palace in Europe, grander and more magnificent than any other private dwelling in the world." Seven years before his death, Flagler extended his railway, now known as the Florida East Coast Railway, from

Biscayne Bay to Key West. In 1913, at age eighty-four, Flagler fell down a flight of stairs in Whitehall. He died on May 20, 1913.

Whitehall was closed down for three years following Flagler's death. Following her marriage to Robert Worth Bingham, Mary Lily visited Whitehall once more. After Mary Lily's death later that year, her niece, Louise Clisby Wise Lewis, came into possession of Whitehall. She sold the beautiful mansion to a group of investors who converted it into a hotel, which operated from 1925 to 1959. Just before Whitehall was to be razed in 1959, Henry Flagler's granddaughter, Jean Flagler Matthews, formed a nonprofit corporation to buy the property. On February 6, 1960, Whitehall was renamed the Henry Morrison Flagler Museum and opened to the public.

Some say that the paranormal activity reported by visitors and staff at the museum is the direct result of the feud that divided the Flagler family into those who approved of Mary Lily and those who did not. Soon after the mansion was turned into a museum, staff members noticed that possessions belonging to different factions of the family could not be placed in the same display case. Some objects vanished, only to reappear in entirely different locations. Occasionally, breakable objects, such as plates, exploded inside their protective covers.

Over the years, other strange occurrences in the museum point to the presence of otherworldly visitors. Doors that have been locked for no apparent reason have been discovered in the museum. On another occasion, someone—or something—upset the lid of a large Japanese vase near the grand staircase. Some even claim that sometimes Mary Lily herself makes an appearance in the museum. Both a curator and a librarian from the Palm Beach County Historical Society saw a woman in a long blue dress carrying a parasol. A female ghost has also been sighted in the ladies' room and the upstairs hall.

The paranormal activity at the Henry Morrison Flagler Museum has dissipated in recent years, not long after John Blades became director. When Blades first heard the ghost tales, he said to himself, "Oh, no. Not another haunting at a historic home." Blades feels that the ghost stories associated with the museum pale in comparison to the history that echoes from every corner of the mansion: "We're keeping alive the spirit of people long gone. In a way, they're more alive than any ghost."

The Henry Morrison Flagler Museum is in Palm Beach, just north of West Palm Beach, Coconut Row at Whitehall Way; phone: 407-655-2833.

Anderson's Corner

Some houses seem to retain the memory of emotionally shocking events from the past, much like the human mind does. Troy Taylor, author of *The Ghost Hunter's Guidebook*, writes, "Often, the mysterious images that are recorded relate to traumatic events that have taken place and that have caused some sort of disturbance (or 'impression') to occur there. This is the reason why so many battlefields, crime scenes and areas related to violence have become famous for their hauntings." For almost thirty years, a rectangular two-story structure in Homestead, Florida, known as Anderson's Corner has been haunted by unsubstantiated stories of domestic strife and, quite possibly, the unquiet spirits of members of the Anderson family.

William Anderson was born September 24, 1877. After arriving in West Palm Beach from Indian Springs, Indiana, in 1898, Anderson found work in Jupiter butchering cattle. In 1900, Anderson moved to Miami and, along with the Charlie Gossman family, became two of the earliest pioneering families in the Silver Palm area. At first, Anderson lived with his sister Flora in a one-room house on Farmlife Road, one-fourth mile above Coconut Palm. Anderson soon found work running the commissary car for the Drake Lumber Company, where he met Atka Harper, a widow with three children. At the time, Atka was running the hotel for the lumber company in Princeton. According to local lore, Mrs. Harper's children hid in a box by the road while Anderson drove up in a buggy to court their mother. As the buggy passed the box, the children moved the box and spooked the horse. The frightened animal bolted down the road with Anderson hanging on for dear life. By the time he finally arrived at Mrs. Harper's house, his clothes were torn and dirty, and he was late.

William Anderson and Atka Harper married in 1911. The couple decided to go into business for themselves, so they purchased five acres for five hundred dollars and hired a shipbuilder by the name of Rawls to build the structure now known as Anderson's Corner. Rawls used sturdy Dale County pine from the Dale County Lumber Company. Anderson's choice of contractor proved to be fortuitous. Because Rawls designed the interior of the upper story like an inverted ship's hull, Anderson's Corner has survived several major hurricanes. The Andersons needed a large home to accommodate their growing brood. William and Atka had five children in addition to Atka's three children.

William and Atka opened a small grocery store on the first level and lived in the second level. The east side of the store sold staples such as beans, flour, sugar, lard, and bacon; the west side had sundries, such as men's work clothes and yard goods. Anderson often brought pioneer families living within a radius of ten miles to community meetings held at the schoolhouse across from the store. Anderson, who was known as "Uncle Will," is remembered by locals as a kindly man who often waved at passersby from the front of the store.

However, period newspaper accounts and court records suggest that all was not well within the Anderson household. Atka filed for divorce from William on April 28, 1936. She moved to a different building on the Anderson property, where she spent the rest of her life. Rumors began circulating that William had left his wife for his stepdaughter, Annie. After the divorce, Annie moved back into the building. She died of a self-inflicted overdose in the 1940s. The oldest of the Harper children, Francis, died in a motorcycle accident. William Anderson remained at Anderson's Corner until he died on February 17, 1961, at age eighty-three.

Anderson's Corner underwent a series of transformations, both during and after William Anderson's lifetime. In 1935, J. Edgar Hoover used Anderson's Corner as his headquarters while searching for a criminal named Cash Kid. The store was in operation until the mid-1930s. In 1936, it was converted into apartments for migrant workers. In 1970, Anderson's Corner was sold to Mr. and Mrs. James Cothron. In the 1970s, the building was once again converted into an apartment complex. Anderson's Corner achieved some notoriety at this time when a Baptist Church filmed a western movie at the site. The building was condemned toward the end of the decade, but efforts by the Cothrons led to its becoming a Dade County Historic Site in 1981. Not long afterward, Joan Green bought Anderson's Corner from the Cothrons. In 1991, she opened a restaurant there called the Harbor House. Nine months later, Anderson's Corner was severely damaged by Hurricane Andrew, and the restaurant went out of business. The property was sold after Green was unable to meet the historical criteria while refurbishing the house.

Anderson's Corner's reputation as a haunted house began in the 1970s when it was used for apartments. A former tenant named Beulah Glenn lived there only two months, but her short stay was long enough to convince her that someone other than she and her family were occupying the downstairs apartment. She said that at night they were frequently awakened by lights that came on by themselves. It was what they heard upstairs, though, that really put their nerves on edge: "We heard people screaming, and chains were dragging. Nobody else lived upstairs . . . The door was padlocked, and it was used for storage. My husband would look upstairs, and nobody was there. We thought it might be neighbor kids playing

tricks, but we would go outside, and nobody was there."
One night, after hearing a girl's voice screaming, "Help!
Help!" Mrs. Glenn decided she had had enough, and the
family moved.

The haunting continued following the destruction
caused by Hurricane Andrew. In January 1994, Scott
Strawbridge, a contractor hired by Joan Green, hired two
Iroquois Indians, David and "Hawk" Hawkins, and a few
other workers to refurbish the house. During this time,
Hawk kept a journal to record his observations. While
they were stabilizing the building with shoring, Hawk
saw a female apparition, in her mid-twenties, in the building. He described her as being five feet tall with long,
light hair. The workers left after two months but returned
in the summer of 1994. In September, Hawk and Dave
often felt the presence of someone standing beside them.
On December 22, the Hawkins brothers were standing
near the walk-through by the kitchen when they heard
the sound of a metal pipe being dropped on the floor
above. They ran upstairs to investigate and found an iron
pipe on the second-level subflooring. Both upstairs doors
had been nailed shut, making it impossible for someone
to sneak inside. A few days later, the brothers heard tap-
ping coming from a mirror. They removed the mirror, but
found nothing inside the four-inch recessed space.

Hawk's unsettling feelings about the house intensified
over time. On several occasions, he saw a badly beaten
woman sitting in a corner. Not long afterward, Hawk

had to fight off a compulsion to kick a ten-ton hydraulic jack onto his brother's head. Walking upstairs, Hawk began to feel what he described in his journal as a "strong sexual presence." When he entered the bath, he had a vision of a young woman being molested by an older man while she was taking a bath. After the older man left the room, Hawk said he was overcome with "a feeling of shame and endless pain." That night, Dave dropped what he was doing and ran outside. Once Dave had regained his composure, he told Hawk that he had been chased out of the house by spirits. Realizing that he could no longer work in a building infested with "bad energy," Hawk performed a cleansing ritual. Minutes before he started, Joan Green was driving over to the site to take pictures. As she walked through the door, Joan was shocked to find a noose tied to the stair railing and smoke wafting through the building. Hawk explained that he was "smudging the structure of spirits." After listening to Hawk's stories about his encounters, Joan showed him an old photograph of the Anderson family. He immediately picked out William and Annie as the two spirits he had seen in the house.

Hawk's ceremony seems to have achieved its purpose. No new occurrences were reported at the site while Joan Green owned Anderson's Corner. Anderson's Corner stands vacant now, a mute relic from Florida's frontier past. But who can say, with absolute certainty, that Anderson's Corner is really empty?

Homestead is near the junction of U.S. Highway 1 and Highway 27 in the southern tip of Florida. Anderson's Corner is located at the corner of Silver Palm Drive and Newton Road.

Boston House

FORT PIERCE

*I*f a private residence stands long enough, chances are good that it will undergo a series of transformations. In every part of the country, old houses have been converted into apartment houses, hotels, law offices, doctors' offices, and libraries. A long history of multiple occupancies in a single building makes it difficult for paranormal researchers to track down the source of a haunting. Such is the case with Boston House in Fort Pierce, Florida.

"Cresthaven," as Boston House was originally known, was built on Indian River Drive next to the courthouse in 1909 by William T. "Big Bill" Jones. Jones, a former railroad engineer, came to Fort Pierce from his native Georgia, where he met the woman who was to become his wife. After his family had increased to five children, Jones decided it was time to build his dream house. When completed, with $6,000 Jones had received in a settlement following a train accident, Cresthaven had five bedrooms, two baths (a luxury in 1909), and elegant Ionic fluted pillars facing Indian River Drive. Jones, a large, "handsome-ugly" man with a great sense of humor, was liked by everyone he met. Although he had built Cresthaven as a showplace suitable for a man who had made it in the world, it eventually became a warm family home, filled with the laughter of children.

On a fatal day in May 1915, an incident occurred in Fort Pierce that changed Big Bill Jones's life forever. The peaceful aura that had settled over Fort Pierce on this beautiful spring day was shattered by the sound of two shots, about a second apart, and then several more shots. One of Jones's sons, Lewis, ran out of the drugstore where he worked as a soda jerk and ran into the alley. On the ground lay Sheriff Dan Carlton; he was killed by U.S. marshal D. J. Disney, who was seen staggering over to a nearby building. The sheriff was carried over to the offices of Dr. Clark. Three minutes after being laid out on the operating table, Carlton died. Disney was taken to a train bound for Miami. Shortly after Carlton died, Big Bill Jones was appointed to the post by Governor Park Trammell. Jones was elected twice before finally resigning in 1920 over a salary dispute.

During the depression, Jones lost Crestview through mortgage in an effort to preserve his grove lands up in Indian River County. For a time, the Neoclassical/Georgian mansion was operated as a bed and breakfast.

Crestview's name was eventually changed to Boston House, probably because of its proximity to Boston Avenue. For a time, Boston House belonged to Jon McCarty, who never lived in it but rented it out for office space. In 1957, Boston House was bought by an engineering firm, now Wood, Beard and Associates. On February 29, 1984, Boston House was purchased for $195,000 by Jafco Corporation of Port Saint Lucie. It became the home of the law offices of attorney Ken Phillips and his partners.

The ghost story associated with Boston House had its origins in the period when it was a bed and breakfast. Mrs. Aleacon Perkins, her husband, and her son Timmy were on vacation when they arrived at Boston House. The next morning, Mrs. Perkins's husband and son went fishing. When her husband and son failed to return at the designated time, Mrs. Perkins alerted the authorities. The next day, her husband's lifeless body washed ashore. Timmy's body was never found.

People familiar with the history of the house claim that the female spirit detected by mediums in later years is the ghost of Mrs. Perkins, who is still searching for her lost son. For many years, the apparition of a woman in a long flowing gown with red hair has been seen looking out the third-floor window toward the Indian River. Legions of coworkers have complained about the flowery odor of perfume wafting through the old building. Psychics invited by former owners of the house have contacted a "presence" within the house. The ghostly figure of a woman has also been sighted standing on a high point of land, staring out over the river.

However, other ghosts might be inhabiting Boston House as well. Over the years, past owners of the house have reported hearing unexplained thumps and manic laughter in the house. One resident occasionally felt searing waves of heat in the old house. Diane Cottem of Palm Beach, who owned the house with her husband, Leonard Cottem, said that she saw a red-haired maiden and a group of Indians sitting in a circle on the lawn. Past owners have also reported seeing images of hanging victims in the house. During a séance, a medium said the house is haunted by the spirit of a wailing woman who was mourning a hanging victim.

Employees working in the law offices housed in Boston House have also reported paranormal activity. Attorney Ken Phillips first became aware that his firm was living with an otherworldly presence immediately after taking possession of Boston House: "We would come in after work and paint or what have you. I began to notice that paintbrushes were not where I left them. My partners noticed the same things, and we just thought others of us were doing it. Only later did we talk about it and find out we weren't responsible."

The Boston House is located at 239 South Indian River Drive in Fort Pierce. It now serves as home to the Phillips and Ziskinder Law Firm; phone: 561-466-8000.

Gilbert's Bar House of Refuge, Hutchison Island

STUART

In the eighteenth and nineteenth centuries, surviving a shipwreck off Florida's east coast was problematic at best. If one were fortunate enough to escape the sinking ship and avoid being drowned in the surf, he then had to contend with a number of other obstacles. Food and water were scarce in most of the coastal areas. Sailors weakened by hunger and injuries were often preyed upon by cougars and bears. After the Civil War, the federal government began responding to complaints made by sailors all over the world. Lifesaving stations called "houses of refuge" were set up every twenty-six miles between Cape Canaveral and Miami. At one time, Florida's east coast was dotted with homey dwellings where one could find food, water, and blankets. They were manned by keepers who earned $450 per year, on the average. The keeper's primary mission was to rescue people who had managed to swim ashore after being shipwrecked. Now, only one remains, Gilbert's Bar House of Refuge on Hutchison

Island. Legend has it that at least one of the former occupants of the old house has managed to survive death itself.

On March 19, 1875, the secretary of the treasury leased a piece of land at Saint Lucie Rocks as a site for a house of refuge. This lonely, barren stretch of rock and sand was named after Don Pedro Gilbert, a nineteenth-century pirate who pillaged ships hung up on the bar. In 1832, Gilbert became the last pirate to be hanged in America. Completed on March 19, 1876, Gilbert's Bar House of Refuge became the last hope for sailors who otherwise would have perished on the beach. On April 19, 1886, the brigantine J. H. Lane was wrecked 14.5 miles north of Jupiter Lighthouse and 5.5 miles south-southwest of Gilbert's Bar Station. All but one of the eight crew members were rescued by the lifesavers. Another significant rescue involved the twelve-man crew of the 767-ton bark George Valentine, who were stranded on October 16, 1904. Seven sailors were saved that day. The station continued in active service under the Coast Guard until 1941 when the navy took it over as a patrol station for the beach. The station ceased operations in 1945 at the end of World War II, but it reopened as a museum in 1955.

This historic outpost of the U.S. Lifesaving Service is quiet now, except for the occasional tourist and the ringing of the telephone. However, some of the employees and volunteers at the station believe that not all of the former residents realize that their services are no longer needed. Cindy Rybovich, who was keeper of the House of Refuge in the 1990s, believes it is haunted by the ghost of Susan Bessey, who lived there from 1890 to 1904: "Mrs. Bessey kept a very nice house. It wasn't the primitive bachelor pad you might think. She would invite people over to tea." Today, the Gilbert's House of Refuge has been restored to reflect the period when the Besseys lived there. Cindy claims that she has never seen the ghost of Mrs. Bessey, but two of her coworkers did. Mark Tamblyn, an environmental researcher, reported seeing the image of a woman in an upstairs window. Assistant keeper Una Wera told Rybovich that on more than one occasion she found "sparkly stuff" on the furniture and floors.

According to the current keeper of the House of Refuge, Katie Rosta, nothing unusual has happened in the museum since she began working there in June 2002. However, this is not to say that the spectral activity in the old station has stopped altogether. In fact, the ghostly manifestations seem to have taken on a different form in the new millennium: "The only thing I have heard is that volunteers who worked there a couple of years ago told stories about smelling cooking in the house. A lot of smells come out of the house. They say that Mrs. Bessey is doing the cooking. She loved to entertain and to cook. A lady told me that when she worked there, she smelled stew and spices cooking early in the morning. I haven't had anyone tell me that they have seen anything. I'm out there almost everyday and haven't smelled or seen any-thing out there at all."

There are at least two explanations for the paranormal occurrences in the Gilbert's Bar House of Refuge. It could be that an extremely exaggerated sense of duty has compelled the spirits of long-dead guardians to keep an eternal watch on the treacherous coastline of Hutchinson Island. On the other hand, if Mrs. Bessey is indeed the apparition who is making her presence known in the life-saving station, an impulse much stronger than duty could be making her stay. For Mrs. Bessey and hundreds of other wives of keepers, the house of refuge was much more than a lifesaving station. It was their home.

Gilbert's Bar House of Refuge is located at Saint Lucie Rocks, two miles north of Gilbert's Bar Inlet. The address is Gilbert's Bar House of Refuge, Hutchinson Island, 301 SE MacArthur Blvd., Stuart, FL 34996; phone: 561-225-1875.

Georgia

17Hundred90 Inn and Restaurant

he 17Hundred90 Inn and Restaurant is Savannah's oldest inn, although only the brick foundation of the building dates back that far. It was destroyed twice in two of the great fires that devastated Savannah in the nineteenth century. The charred timbers above the basement dining room still bear traces of those terrible conflagrations. The garden dining area and kitchen are actually located in a house built in 1820 for Steele White, a Savannah merchant. Thousands of visitors are drawn to the inn because of its period atmosphere and gourmet cuisine. Many, though, visit the 17Hundred90 Inn and Restaurant in the hope that they will meet Savannah's most famous ghost.

The ghost story that is inextricably linked with the 17Hundred90 Inn and Restaurant is the tragic tale of a young girl victimized by love. One version of the legend has it that an elderly merchant imported a child bride named Anna Powers from Ireland. Soon after she arrived

in Savannah, he ensconced her in Room 204 while he
made preparations for their wedding. Just a few days
before her wedding, Anna threw herself from a balcony
into the courtyard below. According to the version told
by Chris Jurgenson, the German-born owner of the old
inn, Anna Powers fell in love with a German sailor who
did not return her affections. As his ship sailed out of
sight down the Savannah River toward the sea, the distraught young woman hurled herself off the balcony.
Regardless of which story is true, there is no doubt in
the minds of many patrons and employees that Anna
Powers's melancholy spirit still haunts the 17Hundred90
Inn and Restaurant.

Most of the haunting activity in the 17Hundred90
Inn and Restaurant has taken place in Anna's room,
Room 204. Apparently, Anna enjoys turning the lights off
and on in Room 204. She also enjoys playing with water.
Guests standing in the bathroom have watched the lava-
tory turn off and on. Other guests have answered the
telephone, only to hear a woman sobbing on the other
end of the line. One guest who unplugged the phone
said that it continued ringing anyway. At least once or
twice a year, guests have had experiences so horrifying
that they run screaming out of Room 204. A good
example is a honeymooning couple who was awakened
by drops of water falling on their faces. The bride was
convinced that the ghost of Anna Powers was standing
over the bed, weeping incessantly. Sometimes, though, six

or eight months will go by with nothing unusual at all taking place in Room 204.

Not surprisingly, entirely new stories about Anna Powers were generated when Rooms 201 and 204 were renovated in the summer of 2002. The crew supervisor said that one of the workers was moving a large piece of furniture in Room 204 in order to unplug an electrical cord when something grabbed his arm and pulled on it. Not long afterward, the foreman had a strange experience in that room. He was changing a shower head when he heard talking in the room. Initially, he assumed that the voices were coming from the hallway. When the volume of the talking increased, he decided to walk into the room and check out the television, but was shocked to find that the television was not on. Suddenly, the television made a whining sound and turned itself on. The supervisor turned off the television and walked into the next room, thinking that the sound might have originated there, but he found nothing. Later, one of the female employees told him that a couple of guests staying in Room 204 had had a similar experience with the television. While they were asleep, they heard the volume of the television get louder and louder. When they looked at the television, they noticed that it had not been turned on. All at once, they heard a clicking sound, and the television came on.

Strange incidents have taken place in parts of the hotel as well. On one occasion, the concierge entered Room 106 to place a bottle of wine on the dresser for a late arrival. As a rule, the door never shuts all the way. This time, though, the door slammed shut, all by itself. Anna Powers's ghost seems to get upset when women enter the kitchen area. One morning, the concierge walked past a stack of large silver serving trays on top of the refrigerator. All at once, one of the trays fell off the refrigerator and landed at her feet. It would have been impossible for one of the trays to simply "fall off" because they were stacked, one inside the other. Anna's presence has been felt in the bar area as well. One night, a waitress was serving ice tea to a group of three young men and three young women. The tea was lukewarm because it had been sitting on the tray for a while. When the waitress set the tray down in the middle of the table, one of the glasses exploded. This sort of thing usually occurs when a beautiful woman is present.

The spirit who haunts the 17Hundrend90 Inn and Restaurant is, in the most basic sense, a poltergeist or "noisy ghost," whose presence manifests itself in violent acts. However, the evidence also matches the definition of an "intelligent haunting," which involves a spirit who interacts with the living. The ghost of Anna Powers appears to be jealous of beautiful women and couples in love. In other words, the spirit of the 17Hundred90 Inn and Restaurant seems to illustrate William Shakespeare's classic line, "Hell hath no fury like a woman scorned."

The 17Hundred90 Inn is located at 307 East President Street, Savannah, Georgia; phone: 912-236-7122.

The William Kehoe House

Some houses seem to scream, "I am haunted," simply because of their age, appearance, and history. Such a place is the William Kehoe House in Savannah, Georgia. This Renaissance Revival-style home was built by William Kehoe in 1892. Kehoe, the owner of an iron foundry, built one of the first fireproof structures in the entire city. Even the ornamentation on the exterior of the house is made of cast iron. After his death around the turn of the century, his wife continued to live in the William Kehoe House for many years. Legend has it that she had asked to be transported to the Catholic cemetery in a very fine conveyance. After her death, though, her casket was placed in a wagon and carted over to the cemetery. In 1910, the Kehoe House became a funeral home. For sixty-five years, coffins were slid in and out of the basement window on the side of the house facing President's Street. A ten-foot section of the curb was removed to facilitate the process. After the funeral home closed in 1975, a syndicate of men bought the Kehoe

House with the intention of turning it into a gentlemen's club, but their plans fell through. In 1992, the present owner spent one million dollars on extensive renovations and opened what has become one of the finest bed and breakfasts in Savannah. The elegant dining room where breakfast is served was, at one time, the funeral home's viewing room. The Kehoe House offers its guests rooms filled with luxurious antique furnishings, fine dining, and, for a fortunate few, an encounter with the supernatural.

Like many haunted inns, the Kehoe House has only a few rooms where ghostly activity has been reported. In the Shannon Suite, a spectral woman in white has made an appearance, but only when the room is occupied by guests of the same gender. Room 201 is usually the last room on the second floor to be rented because it has two single beds. Most people who stay in this room experience the same phenomenon. While sitting on the bed or in a chair watching television, many guests have felt someone come up behind them and rub them very lightly on the back of their head or touch them on their cheek. A guest spending the night in Room 203 claimed to see someone sitting on the edge of her bed at night. On another night, a guest in the same room saw a female apparition writing at the desk. In Room 301, the ghostly figure of a woman in white has also been seen, usually accompanied by the scent of rose water.

Several staff members have reported feeling an unseen presence while they go about their jobs. On one occasion, the female spirit who haunts the Kehoe House showed up in what is probably the spookiest part of the entire inn, the basement. The witness to the ghostly event was a concierge who had worked at the Kehoe House for four years without experiencing anything unusual. Then one evening, she was collecting dirty towels from room to room. She had made three trips downstairs and walked through the basement hallway to the linen closet. On her fourth trip to the basement, she walked down the center stairway and was overcome with a feeling of dread on the bottom step. Goosebumps began popping up on her arms and neck. As she stepped into the basement hallway and turned around, she saw a lady in white, hovering about a foot off the floor at the end of the hall. All the girl could do was stand there, mesmerized, unable to do much more than rock back and forth. Closing her eyes, she finally mustered up enough strength to say, "God, please make her go away!" When she opened her eyes, the ghost was gone. Still shaking, she made her way back up the stairs to the front desk, where she hyperventilated. The young man who was ready to start the next shift found her sitting there, breathing heavily. Only after drinking a cup of coffee laced with cognac was the girl able to calm down.

For the most part, the ghostly visitors in the Kehoe House are "friendly spirits," as some of the comments in the guest book seem to indicate. The ghosts seem to enjoy getting "up close and personal" with the guests and staff. For most people, these odd encounters are nothing more than that. For others, though, their meetings with representatives from "the other side" are a little too personal.

The Kehoe House is located at 123 Habersham Street in Savannah, Georgia; phone: 800-820-1020.

Magnolia Place Inn

SAVANNAH

*t*he Magnolia Place Inn has a fascinating history. The Second Empire house was built in the "Steamboat Gothic" style in 1878 by a cotton broker named Guerard Hayward, a direct descendant of one of the signers of the Declaration of Independence. Hayward died in 1884 after eating some bad oysters. The same year, the family lost much of its fortune in the cotton crash, brought about when boll weevils destroyed most of Georgia's cotton crop. Left with no means of supporting herself or her children, his wife, Pauline Hayward, decided to set herself up as a midwife for women who did not wish to have their children at home. One of the women who delivered a baby there was the mother of Conrad Aiken; he was born there in 1889. The old house was converted into an inn in 1984. One of the inn's most illustrious patrons is John Berendt, author of *Midnight in the Garden of Good and Evil.* Guests at the Magnolia Place Inn might find themselves getting a little closer to history than they are comfortable with.

Staff members over the years have told some strange tales about the old inn. One young woman saw something wet on the first floor, just inside the front entrance. When she looked closer, she noticed a wet footprint. At the time, it was not raining outside. Another time, a maid walked into the sitting room and saw a gentleman in one of the antique chairs, drinking brandy and smoking a cigar. The maid walked upstairs to tell one of the other staff members, and when she returned, the man was gone, but the odor of his cigar remained.

Unexplained occurrences have also taken place in the guest rooms. Several years ago, a man who was doing research in Savannah for a book he was writing on the Civil War came down to breakfast in an agitated state. He claimed that he had seen a Confederate soldier standing by his bed the night before. The man described the soldier as being dirty and ragged. In the downstairs area of the inn, guests have reported cold spots and the feeling of a presence in the room. Some staff members feel that the spirit of Mrs. Hayward is checking in on her children.

Although no one has ever felt threatened by the spirits in the inn, a few people have had frightening experiences there. My wife, Marilyn, and I had such an encounter in the Lafayette Room—Room 304—when we spent the night there on July 24, 2002. We were lying in bed asleep until two o'clock, when Marilyn shook me awake and told me the following story: "I was going to get up out of bed to go to the bathroom when all of a sudden, there was this loud buzzing in the room. It was an electrical kind of noise. Then the hair on the right side of my head kind of stood on end, and the buzzing noise was moving. I tried to wake you up, but I couldn't move my arm. I couldn't go back to sleep. I just lay here. I felt something heavy was keeping me from moving. It was like I was paralyzed. I was scared to death. When I was able to move my head, I noticed that the time was two A.M." Even though both of us were convinced that she had experienced something extraordinary, we were more surprised when I read the following in Laura Foreman's *Haunted Holidays*: "This 19th century building is the site of strange and perhaps ghostly happenings. Water flows mysteriously from a faucet in an empty bathroom, odd noises awake the innkeeper, a guest is unaccountably pinned to a bed in which an old man died 50 years earlier" (149). When I showed the book to Marilyn, she immediately recognized the man's experience in the bed as being strikingly similar to her own.

After conducting additional research into this particular type of interaction between ghosts and sleeping human beings, I found that the phenomenon is not unique to the Magnolia Place Inn. In her book *True Hauntings: Spirits with a Purpose*, ghost investigator Hazel M. Denning told of a young woman who was almost asleep when she sensed another presence in the room. She attempted to look around to see who was there, but she was unable to move. The young woman was so frightened that she tried to call out to her parents, but she could not make a sound. After a few minutes, the paralysis subsided, and she was able to get out of bed. In this case, a psychic determined that the paralysis was caused by the ghost of a young boxer who touched the girl's pressure points so that he could talk to her. Maybe someday a psychic or ghost investigator will find out the purpose behind the nocturnal visitations in the Magnolia Place Inn.

The Magnolia Place Inn is located at 503 Whitaker Street, Savannah, Georgia; phone: 800-238-7674.

Factor's Walk

SAVANNAH

*T*he forty-foot bluff spanning Bay Street in Savannah is now the dividing point between two of the city's main streets. In the nineteenth century when hundreds of bales of cotton were shipped in and out of Savannah every day, cotton brokers, or factors, as they were called back then, had their offices on Bay

Street on the top side of the bluff. On the downside of
the bluff is River Street. A lane called Factor's Walk ran
between the bluff and the buildings. Small walking
bridges arch over Factor's Walk, connecting the second-
and third-story offices with the sidewalks of Bay Street.
Steep stairs and cobblestone ramps leading down to River
Street were built with ships' ballast. In the 1970s, this area
underwent a dramatic face lift. Today, the old buildings
have been converted into city offices, historic inns, and
restaurants. It is said that ghostly remnants from Savannah's
tragic past still linger in the dark recesses of two of the
buildings along River Street.

In the nineteenth century, thousands of slaves toiled
in the cotton warehouses that were once part of the landscape of Bay Street and River Street. The overseers' primary concern was to get as much work out of the slaves as
possible while feeding them just enough to keep them
alive. Loading cotton and lifting heavy crates in Savannah's
sweltering summer heat took its toll on hundreds of
workers. Unlike their counterparts on the plantations, the
slaves in the warehouses had no one to see to their food,
clothing, or medical care. In the winter, slaves were not
allowed to build fires for warmth for fear of igniting the
cotton. Any slave who became seriously ill was probably
doomed to die. Slaves who complained or who tried to
run off were severely beaten and locked up in holding
pens. Those charged with capital crimes, such as rape and
murder, were summarily hanged. For most of the slaves,

Savannah's cotton warehouses along the riverfront were truly hell on earth.

One of these renovated warehouses, the Shrimp Factory at 313 East River Street, is quite possibly haunted by one of these poor souls. The haunting activity in this up-scale seafood restaurant centers around a small room on the second floor that is now used as the liquor room. In the early 1860s, a slave contracted pneumonia and was carried up to this room to recover or to die. With only a threadbare blanket and the clothes on his back for warmth, he shivered in the unheated room for several days before he died, delirious and alone. For years, employees have reported feeling unusually cold in the liquor room, even in the summer. Some have even heard moans in the liquor room, usually during the winter. The ghost, nicknamed "Joe" by the employees, appears to have a playful side. Some waiters have found beer kegs inexplicably opened in the liquor room. Others complain that Joe plays with the light switch. Sometimes, the lights do not turn on at all, and other times, they dim and go out altogether. One longtime waitress who has never seen or heard the ghost is highly skeptical of the stories told by her coworkers. She does admit, though, that having a ghost in the liquor room is handy for keeping out unauthorized persons.

The Savannah Harley-Davidson Shop at 503 East River Street is haunted by a mysterious spirit, undoubtedly that of one of the thousands of slaves who suffered mightily on the riverfront. One young lady who works there is certain that something not of this earth is interrupting her daily routine. Late one afternoon, just before closing time, she saw a white misty shape glide across the second-floor balcony, move down the side stairway, and vanish at the foot of the stairs. A few weeks later, she had another unnerving experience late in the evening involving the wire sculpture of a man and a woman on a Harley-Davidson motorcycle: "I was standing by the cash register staring out the front door when I noticed the wire sculpture rock back and forth. The door and windows were closed, so there was no breeze at all in the store. I locked up early that night. My mother won't even come into the store because she says there are spirits here."

The atmosphere today on Factor's Walk is far different from that encountered by visitors to the area in Savannah's antebellum period. Today, shoppers frequent the stylish shops and restaurants where slaves once carried bales of cotton. Peals of laughter and dinnertime conversation echo in the buildings where the groans of workers once resounded. There are some, however, who believe that the indelible impression left by these sad souls can still be sensed on Factor's Walk.

The Shrimp Factory is located at 313 East River Street, Savannah, Georgia; phone: 912-236-4299.

Savannah Harley-Davidson at City Market can be found at 503 River Street; phone: 912-231-8000.

Tunnel Hill of Chetoogetta Mountain

TUNNEL HILL

ontrary to popular belief, the Civil War did not consist only of a series of carefully staged battles culminating in the loss of thousands of soldiers. The truth is that hundreds of skirmishes erupted in small towns and backwoods areas throughout the South. One of these little-known battles took place at Tunnel Hill in Georgia. On May 9, 1850, the construction of a tunnel through the Chetoogetta Mountain was completed by the Western and Atlantic Railroad. During the Civil War, the tunnel was strategically important to both the Union and the Confederacy. On May 6, 1864, General George Thomas ran into Confederate forces who were defending the hill. The Confederate skirmishers were so drastically outnumbered that they fled without taking the time to damage the tunnel as they had been ordered. This relatively minor skirmish marked the beginning of the Atlanta Campaign. At least five, possibly seven or more, skirmishes were fought here in 1864 and 1865. Although

only a relatively small number of soldiers died in the skirmishes, a much larger number died in a tent hospital set
up in the area to treat soldiers injured at Chickamauga.
The tunnel continued to serve the community after the
Civil War until the "new" tunnel was completed in 1928.
Plans are now underway to turn the tunnel into a park.
Civil War reenactor Ken Sumner recently discovered that
at Tunnel Hill the past sometimes carries over into the
present.

Ken Sumner suspected that something was not
"right" at Tunnel Hill when he detected the smell of
rotting flesh during one of his visits there. "That smell
turned up at various places in the battle site. It smelled
like someone had discarded a dead dog," Sumner said,
"but there were no dead animals in the area as far as I
could tell." Sumner decided it would be fun to look into
the possibility that Tunnel Hill might be haunted. "At
the very least, we would have something to talk about
around the campfire," Sumner said. On March 16, 2002,
Sumner and several members of the Foundation for Paranormal Research (FPR) met at Tunnel Hill to conduct a
scientific investigation there. Later that evening, Sumner
began establishing a personal rapport with one of the
spirits: "The FPR people use a tri-field meter, which is
a detector for electromagnetic fields. They were using it
to detect entities or fields of a suspicious nature. This
thing was sitting in the tent. I walked into the tent, and it
sounded like it was trying to communicate, so I sat down

and started asking questions. It replied that there were three different entities involved. This went on for an hour and a half. This one particular entity—I'm fairly sure his name was Tom Yancey, a Confederate infantry private. When I asked him if he wanted to go outside the tent and have a cup of coffee, he said he did. When he left, the tri-field meter stopped doing strange things. It was quiet for forty or forty-five minutes. Then it kicked back on its own." Sumner immediately realized that he was now in contact with a far different spirit than that of Tom Yancey: "The second entity was an imp of an evil nature. I didn't have anything to do with it. One of the guys actually went in there and talked to it."

Sumner and his group also encountered spectral horses. They smelled horses and horse manure at various spots on the old battlefield. The sound of hoof beats was heard on the road at various times during the day. One horse even revealed itself in an eerie mist that was visible only on the digital cameras: "In the photos we took there, Colonel Thomas Keye's horse, Black Satin, appeared. The pictures taken of mists showed what appeared to be bits and pieces of horse."

Sumner said that he was not the only member of his group who came into contact with strange entities at Tunnel Hill: "My grandson saw two Confederate soldiers there in broad daylight. He described them to me. Two girls with FPR saw Tom Yancey. We've had mist photographs. The mist wasn't visible to the human eye, but it was to the digital camera. Some of our researchers have been clawed in the middle of a field. I've made the mist move back and forth, depending on what I told the entities to do while we've had researchers there. It's been rather eerie."

In 2003, the eighty-five-acre battlefield, the 1845 Clisby-Austin house, and the surrounding wetlands were donated to the citizens of Whitfield County as a green space to be used by Civil War reenactors, some of whom might encounter the same spirits Ken Sumner awakened at Tunnel Hill. Sumner is glad to have met Tom Yancey and the other ghosts of Tunnel Hill: "The ghost research we conducted there at Tunnel Hill ties us back to what happened to our people in the nineteenth century so that they are not forgotten." Sumner does not believe that he and the rest of his group were victims of mass hypnosis or dementia. Civil War reenactors see things that, as he puts it, "your mind tells you are twentieth-century individuals, but your heart tells you they aren't."

To find Tunnel Hill, from I-75, take Exit 138 to Georgia Highway 201. Turn west. After 2.2 miles, continue straight. Eventually 201 turns right. At the "T" intersection, turn right onto Main Street, then left onto Oak Street. Turn left just past the railroad track on Clisby-Austin Street. After the one-lane covered bridge, look for a pull-off on the left.

kentucky

The Bodley-Bullock House

*T*he Bodley-Bullock house has had a long succession of owners since Samuel C. Long constructed the home for Mayor Thomas H. Pindell in 1814. That same year, Pindell sold the house for $10,000 to Thomas Bodley, who had settled in Lexington in 1787. As a clerk of the district court, Bodley had signed an order to swear in Henry Clay as a member of the bar in 1798. Bodley was also a trustee of Transylvania University, Grand Master of the Lexington Masons, and commander of the Lexington Light Infantry. Bodley served as deputy quartermaster general in the War of 1812, and he greeted the Marquis de LaFayette upon his arrival in Lexington in 1825.

Bodley lost his home in the financial crisis of 1819. It was taken over by the Bank of the United States, which rented it to Transylvania in 1828 for President Alva Wood's residence. Bank president John Tilford bought the house for $5,200 in 1837 and sold it to Daniel Vertner, a Lexington businessman, for $15,000. Daniel and his wife, Elizabeth, raised her niece, Rosa Vertner Jeffrey, in their

home. Rosa went on to write *Woodburn*, a novel of
social life in the South. Following Daniel's death in 1861,
the house was used as the headquarters for Confederate
and Union troops during the Civil War. The Civil War
history of the house is recounted in a diary written by a
neighborhood girl, Frances Dallam Peter. In her diary,
entitled *Window on the War*, Peter describes a grand ball
held in the house when it was occupied by officers of the
Union army. Novelist John Fox Jr. also wrote about a
dance at the same federal headquarters in *Little Shepherd
of Kingdom Come*.

In 1865, Mrs. Vertner sold the house to William A.
Dudley for $9,000. Dudley, who was president of the
Louisville and Nashville Railroad, lived there with his
father, Dr. Benjamin Winslow Dudley, until both men
died in 1870. One of the descendants of the Dudley family
who lived in the house was Maria Dudley Short, a trustee
of the Carnegie Library. She was also instrumental in the
construction of the Gratz Park Library in 1905.

In 1912, Dudley's heirs sold the property to Minnie
Barbee Pettit Bullock, wife of Dr. Waller Overton Bullock,
for $11,000. The Bullock family lived in the Bodley-
Bullock house longer than any other owner. Mrs. Minnie
Bullock (1877–1970) was a very civic-minded lady who
participated in the restoration of the Hunt-Morgan
House in Lexington and the Ephraim McDowell House
in Danville. She was also a gardener, a naturalist, and a
member of the Daughters of the American Revolution.

Minnie Bullock's sister, Rebecca Pettit (1869–1936), lived at the Bodley-Bullock House for a while. In the early 1900s, Minnie created the social settlement schools at Hindman and Pine Mountain in eastern Kentucky. Dr. Bullock (1875–1973) was one of the founders of the Lexington Clinic. After Minnie Bullock's death, the Bodley-Bullock House was left in trust to First Security Bank. Since 1984, the old house has been managed by the Junior League of Lexington with a long-term lease.

Despite the fact that so many people have lived in the Bodley-Bullock House down through the years, the haunting activity there is usually attributed to one of the owners, Mrs. Bullock. Gloria List, the administrator/coordinator of the Bodley-Bullock House, recalled a story told to her shortly after she began working there in 1994: "Before I started working here, there was a photographer in Lexington that takes bridal portraits here. . . . He was taking a picture of a bride walking down a staircase. After he developed the negatives, he said you could see the bride and you could see a form of a woman and a little girl standing next to her. He said you could see it so clearly. After I started working here, I called him and asked him if he could locate the picture. He said if I knew the name of the bride, he could look it up, but I didn't know who it was. There was a little girl who played in the grassy park area here a lot, and she used to come over and talk to Mrs. Bullock. That's who the ghost is supposed to be, the little girl and Mrs. Bullock."

Ms. List believes that Minnie Bullock's personal likes and dislikes are revealed in some of the paranormal activity inside the house. One such incident was reported by a young woman who set up one of the many weddings that are held at the Bodley-Bullock house: "She said that right at the end of the evening, it was getting kind of late. It was time for everybody to be out of the house. There were a lot of people lingering in the entrance foyer, and all at once, the lights started going on and off like somebody was flipping the light switch. It wasn't just a little twinkle of the light. It was off and on, off and on, four times. It was like Mrs. Bullock was tired of everybody being here. She was a real stern teetotaler-type lady. She didn't like parties. In her will, she stipulated that there would be no drinking ever in the house. So they had to go back to the will and change it so that we can serve alcohol during weddings."

Apparently, Mrs. Bullock's personality also manifested itself during a meeting the Junior League held in the boardroom upstairs: "There's a big chandelier that hangs over the conference table. And they were talking about fundraising and maybe having a garage sale in the yard. And as soon as they mentioned doing this, the lights started shaking and the table shook a little bit. They laughed because they thought that was Mrs. Bullock's way of showing that having a garage sale wasn't the proper thing to do. She wouldn't have approved of it."

In December 21, a scientific investigation of the Bodley-Bullock House was conducted. Patti Starr and five other "ghost hunters" tried to collect visual/audio evidence of paranormal energy in the house. Starr's electromagnetic field detector registered very strong readings around Minnie Bullock's wheelchair. Starr also felt a "strong pull" toward Minnie's snow-covered flower garden on the north side of the house. After returning inside, Starr focused her attention on and around the Christmas tree. Although no one present saw or heard anything unusual that night, Starr's photographs showed a tiny grayish orb floating near the ceiling not far from the Christmas tree angel. In addition, one of the tape recorders picked up a gruff voice uttering something that sounded like "Tree!" Starr believed this was the spirit's way of saying that he was near the Christmas tree.

Of course, the Bodley-Bullock House has much more to offer tourists than a resident ghost. Aside from the garden, which has been restored to its original master plan, the house features the Bullocks' snuff bottle collection, an early Kentucky textile collection, a silver collection, period portraits, and pieces of Dr. Bullock's sculpture collection. Most of the time, Ms. List does not think about the ghost at all. In her nine years at the Bodley-Bullock House, she has never heard any of the spectral sounds such as ghostly footsteps reported by other staff members and guests. It is a different story after the sun goes down, though: "I'm not afraid to work here. I've been here every day for nine years. People say she [the ghost] likes me because I take care of the house. I'm not nervous at all in the daytime,

The Old Talbott Tavern

but at night when I close up the house, I get out as fast as I can. It [the house] is big and really creepy. It just gives me the willies."

The Bodley-Bullock House can be found at 200 Market Street in Lexington, Kentucky; phone: 859-259-1266.

The Old Talbott Tavern

BARDSTOWN

Built in 1779, the Old Talbott Tavern is the oldest western stagecoach stop still in business today. Originally known as the Newman House, the old inn has had a number of famous guests over the years, including King Louis Phillipe, Daniel Boone, General George Rogers Clark, Abraham Lincoln, John James Audubon, and General George S. Patton. Of all the celebrities who have visited the inn in the past two hundred years, none have had more of a lasting impact than Jesse James. According to one local legend, James often stayed at the tavern while visiting his cousin Donnie Pence, the local sheriff. During one visit, James became drunk and fired his pistol at imaginary birds flying around the room. On another visit, James decided to make his presence known by shooting at murals painted by King Louis Phillipe and his brothers. Bullet holes from both incidents still remain as proof of James's wild nature. Over the years, guests and staff have discovered that not only can they get in touch with history at the Old Talbott Tavern, but that sometimes history touches back.

Like many haunted places, the Old Talbott Tavern has a tragic past. After purchasing the tavern in 1886, George Talbott set about to make a good home for himself and his new bride. The Talbott's had twelve children, most of whom suffered from a variety of illnesses. Four children died during the same winter. A few months later, the oldest child died after falling down the stairs. Not long afterward, the oldest daughter hanged herself after a failed love affair. George himself died in the inn in 1912. Soon thereafter, his widow changed the name to the Talbott Hotel.

The Old Talbott Tavern's reputation stems from stories told by locals, guests, and employees. According to longtime employee Doug Owens, haunted activity in the tavern is an everyday occurrence. "Little simple things happen around here all the time, lanterns coming on by themselves and chairs moving. Ink pens will disappear. Silverware will disappear and then reappear in the strangest places." Occasionally, guests report actually seeing a spectral figure. "What everybody sees is an image in black.

It has bold or brass on the chest, and there is no face. The phantom has been seen all over the place. Guests have seen him in the rooms and in the hallways. He has also been seen in the kitchen and the basement."

A few years ago, a former bookkeeper identified the male spirit. One night while closing up, she was on her way up the stairs to deposit the day's receipts in the safe when she saw a strange man in long coat walk across the landing. At almost the same moment, the cook saw the same thing. The women became concerned because, to their knowledge, all of the guests had left the building. As they walked up the stairs, they heard the back door of an upper room close. When they walked through the room and opened the back door, they saw the man walk down the hall and leave through the fire escape door. By this time, the manager had joined in the pursuit. Thinking that the man had probably run down the fire escape, she opened the door. To her surprise, he was standing on the landing. Suddenly, he turned around, laughed, and dematerialized. Three weeks later, the bookkeeper was watching a television program about Jesse James. When a photograph of James appeared on the screen, she exclaimed to her husband, "That's the man I saw!" Since then, employees at the tavern have referred to the specter as the ghost of Jesse James.

The Old Talbott Tavern is also home to a female ghost. One young couple left in the middle of the night because of an unnerving experience they had had in their bedroom. They were both awakened by the ghostly form of a lady in white standing over their bed. After staring at the terrified couple for a few moments, she turned around and floated through a nearby window. Sharing the night with a ghost was not what the young couple had in mind when they registered at the Old Talbott Tavern. The lady in white has also been seen during the day in the Colonial Dining Room. When employees follow her into the room, she is nowhere to be found. She has been described as having wavy brown hair and wearing a long white dress in the style of the early 1800s.

In 1998, the Old Talbott Tavern was changed forever by a devastating fire that broke out on March 7. The fire gutted the second floor, taking with it many pictures, rugs, and antique furnishings dating back to the 1700s. While the tavern was being renovated, construction workers found a sub-basement, underground tunnels, and stairways leading nowhere. Amazingly, the murals and the bullet holes Jesse James fired into the wall of his room survived the blaze. The spirits in the tavern remain as well, according to Doug Owens: "The fire made the activity way, way more obvious. Quite a few people who have stayed here recently have sent us photographs with orbs in them." The attention generated by the increased frequency of ghostly manifestations has been good for the Old Talbott Tavern. "The Food Channel came up here a couple of years ago and did a special. We have been featured several times on the Food Network and also on the Travel Channel. We are ranked the thirteenth most haunted inn in the U.S. We are very proud of it."

Bardstown is thirty-five miles southwest of Louisville on U.S. Highway 31E/150. The address of the Old Talbott Tavern is P.O. Box 565, 107 West Stephen Foster, Bardstown, KY 40004; phone: 502-348-3494.

The Hunt–Morgan House

LEXINGTON

Known historically as Hopemont, the Hunt-Morgan House was built by John Wesley Hunt in 1814. The Federal-style residence has many distinctive features, including a Palladian window and a large spiral staircase in the front entranceway. Hunt earned his fortune in the mercantile business shortly after Lexington was founded. Before long, he became the first millionaire west of the Alleghenies. Other notable personalities have lived at the Hunt-Morgan House. Hunt's grandson, John Hunt Morgan, was a Confederate general. His daring raids and utter disregard for danger earned him the nickname of "Thunderbolt of the Confederacy." John Hunt Morgan's son, Dr. Thomas Hunt Morgan, was born in the house in 1865. As a result of his pioneering work in genetics, Dr. Morgan won the Nobel Prize. He is still the only Kentuckian to have received that honor. In 1955, the Foundation for the Preservation of Historic Lexington and Fayette County was formed to save the Hunt-Morgan House. Once the house was saved, the organization restored it to its 1814 appearance. Not only is the Hunt-Morgan House an interpretive museum illustrating the lifestyle of nineteenth-century affluence in Kentucky, but it also contains the Alexander T. Hunt Civil War Museum. Another artifact from the old home's antebellum past might be the spirit of a faithful slave named Betty.

Betty, whose real name was Bouviette James, was nursemaid to the Morgan children, whom she loved very much. Mrs. Morgan treated Betty more like a friend than a servant. Knowing how the Morgans felt about the Confederacy during the Civil War, Betty became an ardent supporter of the "Southern Cause" during the Civil War. She is said to have stood on the corner of Main Street and offered Confederate soldiers a glass of ice water or lemonade from a silver pitcher. Aunt Betty died not long after the end of the Civil War. Befitting a beloved member of the Morgan family, Aunt Betty's funeral was held in the house. Her casket was placed in the parlor of the house. Four of the surviving Morgan sons—Charlton, Calvin, Richard, and Key—and brother-in-law Basil Duke served as pallbearers. She is buried in the Hunt family plot at the Lexington Cemetery.

The inscription on her tombstone reads, "Bouviette, Ever Faithful."

Legend has it that Betty's affection for the Morgan family even transcended the grave. The story goes that one night a nurse was sitting up with one of the Morgan children who was deathly ill. After a few hours, the nurse nodded off to sleep. All at once, she was awakened by the sound of someone humming a nursery tune. Rubbing her eyes, the woman could not believe what she saw. A black woman wearing a colorful turban and red leather shoes was sitting by the boy's bedside and stroking his forehead. As the nurse stood up and walked over to the woman, she vanished.

The next day, the little boy's condition took a turn for the worse, and he died. The nurse told no one about the boy's ghostly visitor the night before. Then several months later, she finally told Mrs. Morgan about the strange experience in her son's bedroom the night before his death. The grieving woman's face brightened when she heard the news because Aunt Betty had always shown up when one of her children needed her. Mrs. Morgan took Aunt Betty's appearance at her dying son's bedside as a sign that she would continue to look after the Morgan children in heaven, just as she had done on earth. When the nurse asked Mrs. Morgan about the red shoes, she replied that Aunt Betty loved bright colors, especially the color red. On several occasions, she mentioned that she would love to have a pair of red shoes. During the Civil War, John

Hunt Morgan remembered Aunt Betty's words. On one of his visits home, he presented her with a pair of red shoes. She seems to have treasured the gift so much that she continued wearing her red shoes even after death.

The antebellum homes and public buildings that still stand today are monuments, not only to a genteel lifestyle that is long gone, but also to a race of people who made that lifestyle possible. The important role played by African American artisans, fieldhands, and house servants is evident everywhere in the South, but no more so than in the homes of the very rich. The ghost story associated with the Hunt-Morgan House survives because it demonstrates the devotion that servants like Aunt Betty gave the families they served.

The Hunt-Morgan House is located at 201 North Mill Street, Lexington, Kentucky; phone: 859-233-3290.

White Hall

RICHMOND

White Hall in Richmond, Kentucky, is really a house within a house. The original structure, Clermont, was built in the Georgian style in 1798–1799 by General Green Clay. Clay was a very wealthy man whose holdings included taverns, distilleries, farms, and a ferry across the Kentucky River. The emancipationist Cassius Marcellus Clay inherited what he called "the old building" from his father, and he placed a new brick building above and around the existing Clermont in the 1860s. Clay's wife, Mary Jane Clay, supervised the construction of White Hall while Clay was in Russia. The renovation, designed in the Italianate style by renowned architect Thomas Lewisnki, is simple in design. One of its most unusual features includes a central heating system fed by two basement fireboxes. Whitehall was also the first house in the region to incorporate indoor plumbing. While Cassius Clay was away during the Civil War, Mrs. Clay saved her home from destruction by southern forces by allowing Union troops to bivouac on her property. White Hall remained in the Clay family for several decades following the death of Cassius. In 1967, it was purchased by the state of Kentucky and restored through the efforts of Governor Louie B. Nunn and his wife, Beula. Now a Kentucky Historic Site, White Hall might still be home to the spirit of one of the mistresses of the house, a woman who is reluctant to depart her beloved home.

Curator Lashe Mullins believes that White Hall is haunted by the ghost of Cassius Clay's first wife, Mary Jane Clay: "We have a lady who walks around on the second floor. They call her the Lady in Black, but she changes her dress color. She's been in blue and yellow—a lot of different colors. She stays in the back hallway on the second floor where the bathrooms are. She goes from one bedroom in the new section of the house all the way down to the old section of the house."

Ms. Mullins does not believe all of the sightings that are reported to her, but she does put a lot of credence in two of them. One person who saw the ghost was a former housekeeper at the mansion: "She said she was giving a tour one day, and she happened to look through a doorway and she saw the back end of a black hoop skirt go down the stairs. And at the time, our inventory of tour guide outfits didn't include a black hoop skirt."

The second sighting that Ms. Mullins believes is true involved her husband. In 1994, he saw the Lady in Black on the third floor while he was giving a tour. "He happened to look up, and he could see her from the torso up," Mullins said. "When he ran up there to investigate, there wasn't anybody there. On the third floor, a tour was going on at the time, and that tour guide didn't see anything. Since then, nobody has really seen her."

Even though the Lady in Black is rarely seen, Mullins says that all of the staff members at White Hall are afraid to work there at night: "Most of what happens here is not the sighting of something physical, but more like noises and smells. I've smelled candle wax burning. We're not supposed to light candles in the house because it's a fire hazard. I've smelled perfume when there was nobody else in the house at the time, and I've smelled bourbon before. I've heard people walking around upstairs when there was no one else in the house. The oddest thing that ever happened to me is [hearing] sounds like someone took a huge wardrobe and slammed it down on the floor and dragged it from place to place, but when you investigate it, it stops. You go around and look, and nothing's been moved. That's the one thing I cannot explain away." Ms. Mullins's husband and a secretary have heard spectral music playing in the old house. "That's really interesting," she said, "because the second wife of the man who owned the house owned a music box, and he made her get rid of it because he didn't like it." Apparently, the poor woman's ghost is enjoying in death one of the pleasures that was denied her in life.

Another eerie sound that torments staff and visitors alike is the murmur of human voices. In the early 1980s, three tour guides were talking in the powder room when they heard soft voices coming from the vents. The three women armed themselves with knives and forks and walked downstairs to the basement area, but they found no one. Lashe Mullins said on another occasion, a guide was changing into her costume when she heard male laughter. No males were present at the time.

Mysterious lights have been seen in the house as well. In the late 1960s when restoration on White Hall began, guards spending the night in a nearby trailer reported watching a single candlelight moving from window to window in the second-floor master bedroom. Every time the guards entered the house to investigate, they found nothing. Lashe Mullins's cousin also saw a strange light in the master bedroom while he was plowing the field surrounding the mansion at dusk. He glanced up and saw a human form outlined by a light standing in the one of the master bedroom windows. He assumed that the light was provided by an automatic timer and that the strange figure was a bedpost. He found out the next day, though, that there are no automatic timers in White Hall.

Even the guide ropes suspended from brass poles have behaved strangely inside White Hall. Lashe Mullins said that one morning in 1995, she walked up to the Blue Room to change into her costume. When she reached the top of the stairs, she noticed that the guide ropes in the doorways of the Blue Room and the Brutus Room were swinging back and forth. There was no breeze in the house at the time. Later that day, a coworker told Lashe that this happens all the time.

Lashe Mullins has a standard reply for people who ask her about the ghost: "Most of the time when people ask me if the house is haunted, I won't say it is. I'll say, 'Sometimes,' because the incidents are so few and far between, and they seem so normal when they happen. I'm not the type who goes around saying, 'There's a ghost around every corner.' I just don't believe it."

White Hall is located at 500 White Hall Shrine Road, Richmond, Kentucky; phone 859-623-9178.

Louisiana

The 1891 Castle Inn

NEW ORLEANS

At the beginning of the nineteenth century, New Orleans was one of the wealthiest cities in the United States. Tycoons and entrepreneurs who made their fortunes in cotton, sugar, and timber constructed elegant Greek Revival mansions in the Garden District to show off their wealth and to outdo their neighbors. This posh residential area derives its name from the beautiful gardens that flourish in the layers of rich black silt deposited by the Mississippi River. One of these Gilded Age showplaces is the Castle Inn. Built in 1891, this 9,500-square-foot bed and breakfast offers visitors nine suites and rooms. Most of the year, the scent of Confederate jasmine wafts through the rooms, notable for their ten-foot-tall windows and thirteen-foot-high ceilings. The old house has been run as a hotel for around fifty years. However, the ghostly activity that attracts—and thrills—visitors from across the country is a fairly recent development.

Douglas Parker realized that the 1891 Castle Inn was not a run-of-the-mill hostelry soon after he took over in 1998. Before long, stories started to circulate about unexplained encounters in darkened rooms and halls. A number of these experiences have been recorded in the guest book. On September 24, 2002, one guest wrote, "We opted to sleep with the lights on that night . . . I heard the sound of someone moving furniture all over the house, like my friend the two nights before. I also began to sense someone was watching us in the room, but hadn't seen anyone. At 1:30 A.M., my friend and I woke at the exact same moment and felt an immense presence in the room. It was much larger than the presence of a human. During this feeling, I had the sensation of a soft caress on my foot and up my leg, followed by fingers caressing my scalp and hair. I couldn't think about sleeping the rest of the night but continued to have the sensation someone was watching me until about 4:30 A.M. At that point, all noises died out."

On July 15, 2002, another guest had a similar close encounter with the spirit world: "We spent three nights in the Jazz Emporium Room and two nights in the Gothic Sanctuary, Room 10. On the second night, Judy, my partner, was awakened with a start as the bed began moving. Then she felt someone, or thing, sit on the bottom of the bed. She woke me up because at first she thought it was me turning in the bed. I missed it all. At first she was afraid and wanted to turn on the light so she could use the bathroom. In the Gothic Sanctuary our radio kept turning itself off as if someone was pushing a snooze button. I checked it all out. One night the light came on by itself. The last night we left the ceiling fan on in the adjoining room only to find the next morning that it was turned off. Yes, it's true—something else lives in this house too!"

A ghost hunter who stayed at the hotel on June 23–25, 2002, was not disappointed by what he found there. "Yesterday, we left our key in the room and the door locked automatically. After arguing, I went to get an extra set. When I arrived back at the room, the door was wide open, and the light was on. Kinda spooky. Later that night I detected the smell of tobacco around the stuffed giraffe. When I finally got to bed, I kept hearing humming outside our door. The dog heard it too and kept staring at the door. I went earlier to the door when [I heard] scratching sounds outside the door. I went to sleep with a necklace on and awoke to find it on the table next to the couch on top of my camera. When I awoke the next morning, both my and my brothers' shoes were arranged in a pattern on the floor."

On August 1, 2001, two guests discovered the playful side of the spirits of the 1891 Castle Inn: "The first day our TV kept coming unplugged. We'd leave, and it would be unplugged when we returned. This happened a total of three times. The second night was amazing and frightening at the same time. We saw this little girl by the stairway. My wife saw the male black ghost once or twice that night. So we finally got to sleep around four A.M.

Oh, yeah, we also heard steps running up and down our stairs. No one else was staying on our side [of the mansion] that night. Around six A.M., we heard a little girl giggling. The final thing happened after we brought some food home from a large dinner and Aly and I decided to reheat it. That was when we found our gift cards in the microwave! Now I assure you, being the type of person I am, I always know where things are. They were in my wallet no more than an hour before. Then they ended up in our microwave. Is this house haunted? I would say yes, unless, of course, I was drinking that night—which I wasn't."

The ghosts at the 1891 Castle Inn have also revealed themselves through unexplained noises, usually at night. On February 24, 2003, a woman spending the night in Room 11 heard someone hammering a nail, "at first tentatively, then very emphatically. When I looked at my watch, it was 1:30 A.M. The banging appeared to come from the alcove in the window. Last night in Room 5, there were more sounds, heavy furniture being moved—not carry-on luggage, but something like armoires." Two years earlier on March 30, 2001, a husband and wife were awakened by the sounds of steel balls banging together for a few minutes. "I heard it one more time an hour later. Then on March 31 at 12:30 A.M., we heard a whooshing sound in the hall, almost like an aerosol can going off. I'm not sure what it was."

On January 25, 2000, a guest got an even better look at the male ghost in Room 12. "The first night we were in Room 12. I had a dream that there was a man in our room sitting on the couch. He had caramel-colored skin, black hair, dark eyes. I think he was wearing something tan colored. And he was cute! I talked to Wynette, and she said that sounded like the description of the ghost, so maybe I wasn't dreaming. The next night, I was awakened by a man's voice in my ear. He was talking in a different language—French, Spanish—I'm not sure. I was half-asleep, and he scared me. [Two nights later], I woke up to hear someone singing in our room. Kim, my friend, heard it too. After that, we asked him to leave us alone, and he did. Neither one of us had been getting enough sleep because of him."

With evidence supplied by ghost researchers, "readings," and testimonials of guests, Parker has identified one of the ghosts at the 1891 Castle Inn as a light-skinned black man who worked as a manservant. He was a fairly sophisticated man who was fluent in several languages. The manservant was also a very outgoing individual who loved wine, women, and music. Tragically, after falling into bed and sleeping off the effect of the night's revelry, he accidentally set his room afire, either by smoking in bed or knocking over a heating pot. He was so inebriated that he failed to wake up when the fire started, and he died from smoke inhalation. The owners of the 1891 Castle Inn feel that his spirit haunts the mansion because it is his rightful place as a gentleman's gentleman, not the servants' quarters. The unearthly whistling and coughing that resound through the hallways is usually credited to him. The ghostly manservant has also been blamed for playing with the radio, lights, televisions, and ceiling fans. According to the staff, his ghost is probably responsible for hiding objects in the hotel. Most likely, he is the "translucent man" who is occasionally seen in mirrors and out of the corner of guests' eyes.

Stephanie Ruiz, who runs the 1891 Castle Inn with Doug Parker, says that her brother caught a glimpse of the illusive manservant one afternoon: "We went out to dinner. We left my mom and my brother here. He said he was in the bathroom, and he turned around to throw something in the trash can, and he saw something out of the corner of his eye. He said a man was standing in the doorway staring at him. When my brother looked up, he was gone. My brother then started washing his hands, and the man was standing there again. He said, 'I ran all the way up the stairs. I was convinced there was some-body there.'" A few minutes later, Stephanie's brother went back downstairs where his mother was waiting. Her mother could tell by the look on her son's face that something terrible had happened to him. "My mother said, 'I was sitting over here [pointing to one side of the parlor], and he was sitting over there, and all of a sudden, we both got the goose bumps. The room got freezing cold.' When Doug and I came home, I asked my brother to describe the figure, but he couldn't. He said the man appeared 'in the blink of an eye' and was gone. My

reserved

brother is thirty-eight years old. He's not some little twelve-year-old kid. I believe him."

Stephanie had her own encounters with the ghost soon after moving into the basement apartment in January 2003: "For several days, I couldn't sleep. Then one night, it was like my feet wouldn't go all the way down [under the covers]. It felt like somebody was sitting at the foot of the bed. Then, all of a sudden, my feet slid under the blanket." On another occasion, Stephanie went into the bathroom to put on makeup while Doug was taking a nap. "I walked out of the bathroom," she said. "He finally woke up and went into the bathroom. Then he came out and asked, 'Did you put this mirror in here?' I said, 'No.' I looked, and this full-length antique mirror that was sitting on the floor was standing on the chair. It felt like [a scene from the movie] *Poltergeist*. I said, 'Doug, you put that there.' He said, 'No, I just woke up. Do you think I'm going to put that mirror on the chair just so that I can hear you scream?'" Stephanie added that several times when she has walked down the stairs from the third floor, she has heard creaking sounds, as if someone is following her.

The lascivious side of the manservant usually manifests itself when an attractive woman is staying at the 1891 Castle Inn. On March 11, 2003, a woman and her boyfriend were asleep in one of the rooms when the television turned on by itself. When they awoke, they discovered that the television screen was blank, and the sound was moving from the television to the clock radio and back to the television. A few nights later at 4:30 A.M., the woman's boyfriend felt a rush of energy surge into his body and hold him down into the bed. All at once, the ghost appeared at the foot of the bed. He was a tall man in a black coat, and he was smoking a cigar. "He pointed to me while I was sleeping," the woman said, "and nodded his head. David then asked him not to hurt us, and he nodded his head again. The ghost kept nodding and pointing at me until David asked him if he thought I was beautiful. He nodded his head again like he approved . . . David then waved, and the ghost waved back. After that, we asked him nicely to leave us alone, and he has. We thanked him for coming in and saying 'Hi' and giving us our space."

The ghost also seems to enjoy disturbing women when they are taking a bath or a shower. On April 3, 2001, a woman was in the bathtub reading a book when she heard the doorknob turn. "The doorknob creaked open about a foot," she said. "I thought it was my husband coming in, so I looked up, and the door promptly slammed shut. I got out of the tub and opened the door. My husband was asleep on the bed. I decided to lay down on the bed for a while. Fifteen minutes later, I was awakened by someone shaking the headboard of the bed back and forth. If they wanted my attention, they sure got it." On June 23–25, 2002, a woman and her husband spent their honeymoon in the 1891 Castle Inn. On June 24, the woman was taking a bath when she heard three knocks on the bathroom door. "Thinking that it was my husband, I called, 'Come in,' three times. Then I heard the knocks again. This time I yelled louder. Finally, my husband heard me calling. He said he was not knocking on the door, nor did he hear anything."

Parker says that the inn is also home to the ghost of a little girl who drowned in a small pond on the former grounds of a local plantation before it was subdivided. Wearing a white dress, the small apparition scours the neighborhood in search of her mother. Apparently, she believes that her mother might be residing in the 1891 Castle Inn. The little girl is probably responsible for turning the water in the restrooms on and off. She also is the ghost who touches women on the leg, bounces up and down on the beds, and runs up and down the hallways. On April 3, 2001, a guest named Jerry reported seeing a child in his room who was "laughing and pointing at me all night, a little girl, I think." On December 21, 2002, a couple attempted to communicate with the spirit of the little girl in Room 4 by means of a ouija board. "The ouija was full of life. It moved around the board at full-speed, as if it was anxious to talk to us. We not only talked to a ghost named George, but we also met D.E., the initials of the little girl's name, possibly."

My wife, Marilyn, and I stayed in the Jazz Emporium Room the night of May 18, 2003, in the hope of experiencing some of the ghostly activity that has been recorded in the guest books, such as the shaking of the bed and the moving of objects like keys and television remotes from one place to another. Unfortunately, we spent a very uneventful night in the room. However, shortly after we arrived at eleven A.M., we turned off the lights in the room and went to lunch at Wendy's on St. Charles Street. When we returned an hour later, the little lamp by the side of the bed was turned on. We found out later that the maid had not been in the room while we were gone.

After Parker became convinced that the bed and breakfast was haunted, he asked the previous owners if they had encountered anything and was surprised to find that they had not. Nevertheless, the large number of guests and staff members who have seen and heard strange things has convinced Parker that there is indeed something in his establishment, something otherworldly. He says that his "best" encounters have come from guests who did not know that the inn was haunted and who have nothing to prove or gain by their stories. Parker added that most of the haunting activity takes place on the third floor at three A.M. While it is true that some "quaint" inns do fabricate hauntings as a marketing gimmick, one gets the impression from the guest book that this is not the case with the Castle Inn.

The Castle Inn is located at 1539 Fourth Street in New Orleans; phone: 504-897-0540.

The Old State Capitol

At first glance, the Old State Capitol in Baton Rouge seems to be a medieval castle miraculously transported from the pages of a Gothic novel. Like many southern capitols, the old building suffered greatly during the Civil War. The Old State Capitol has undergone several periods of renovation over the years and is now a National Historic Landmark. Although the Old State Capitol no longer resembles what Mark Twain jokingly referred to as a "whitewashed castle, with turrets and things," it still projects a somewhat foreboding appearance. Some staff members at the Old State Capitol are convinced that the old building's spooky exterior makes it a suitable haven for the spirits who reside inside.

The Old State Capitol was designed in 1847 by architect James Harrison Daikin. Construction was completed in December 1849 at a total cost of $396,000. On January 21, 1850, the legislature opened its regular session in the new capitol building. In January 1861, members of the secession commission voted to secede from the

Union. After Baton Rouge was captured by Federal forces in 1862, the capitol became a barracks and, for a short time, a Confederate prison. During the Federal occupation of Baton Rouge, the seat of government moved to Opelousas and later to Shreveport. On December 28, 1862, Union soldiers accidentally started a grease fire on the ground floor. Local firemen quickly extinguished the fire, but during the night, the fire erupted again, gutting the entire building. After the Civil War, the Old State Capitol was nothing more than a charred ruin. Following the constitutional convention of 1879, the capital was moved back to Baton Rouge, and the Old State Capitol was completely renovated. Architect William A. Freret added a fourth floor and four square towers on the center and east sides of the capitol. He also installed six cast-iron turret caps to the exterior and a cast-iron spiral staircase to the interior. In 1882, construction was completed, and the legislature once again met in the Old State Capitol. Eventually, the gaudy turrets had to be removed because of their extreme weight.

The Old State Capitol was the site of many heated debates over the years. The final controversy to be argued in the building was the impeachment of Governor Huey Long in 1929. The house voted for impeachment, but the senate refused to remove him from office. Long's hatred for the scene of his public humiliation simmered. He began campaigning for the construction of a new, sky-scraper capitol. On May 16, 1932, the Old State Capitol itself became the subject of debate during a terrible storm. The legislature voted to replace the capitol, some say, because Long placed all the people voting against his proposal under the leaks in the roof. The Old State Capitol began falling into disrepair soon after the new capitol was dedicated on May 16, 1932. In 1937-38, it underwent a $50,000 WPA renovation. Workers were appalled by the damage inflicted on the old building by bats, pigeons, and vandals. In 1978, the Old State Capitol was named a state commemorative area under the Louisiana Department of Parks. Actual construction began in 1992. In 1994, the Old State Capitol was reopened at a gala black-tie reception attended by Governors John McKeithen, Dave Treen, and Buddy Roemer. Thanks to the efforts of women like Mrs. J. W. Tucker, Mrs. Irving Dameron, and Elise Rosenthal, it is now a museum housing exhibits of historic importance to the state.

One of the women who currently works in the building is Freddie Deblieux. According to Ms. Deblieux, the ghost who haunts the Old State Capitol is the spirit of a state senator named Pierre Couvillon: "He died of a heart attack in 1851 at the age of forty-seven. It was two months before the 1852 legislative session began. He was distraught over some legislators trying to bilk the state out of millions of dollars. On the opening day of the session, he was not able to come here. His motto was, 'The government should serve the people. The people shouldn't have to serve the government.' And so we feel his spirit is still walking the halls of the Old State Capitol." Between 1834 and 1844, Couvillon tried to reform the state's corrupt banking system. As a result of his personal crusade, some of Louisiana's most unsavory bankers were put out of business. Most of the time, Couvillon was a kind man who enjoyed storytelling and showed resentment only to those who opposed him or who betrayed the public trust. In fact, an early biographer said that the senator died in a rage at home in Avoyelles Parish after finding out that some of his fellow legislators had benefited financially at the taxpayers' expense.

Although Senator Couvillon has been traditionally identified as the ghost of the Old State Capitol, Ms. Deblieux believes that it could be the ghost of another historical figure: "I have written quite a bit on Henry Watkins Allen, who planted the Ginko tree in 1857 right outside the west wing of the Old State Capitol. He put himself in exile in Mexico during the Civil War. He was gravely injured during the Civil War. When he went to Mexico, he only lived there two or three years before he died. He was buried in Mexico. Then his friends and relatives raised money to bring his corpse to New Orleans, where he was buried. He was [later] brought back to Baton Rouge and was buried here in 1885 right by the tree he planted."

Tourists have reported a number of sightings in the Old State Capitol over the years. Some visitors have felt the presence of people from the 1700s and the 1800s.

Some have smelled cigar smoke. Others say they have heard the swishing of the women's long dresses. "They can picture people," Ms. Deblieux says. "It's just like time has taken them back two hundred years." One man paid for his tour, walked down the hall a short ways, and ran back to Freddie Deblieux. She said that the hair on his head and arms was standing straight up. "There's somebody in the capitol who does not want me in here," he told Ms. Deblieux. She refunded his money, and he left in a great hurry.

Staff members at the Old State Capitol are also treated to an occasional visit from "the other side." One of these "lucky few" was a security guard named Ivy Christy, who watched as upstairs motion detectors tracked something from room to room. She began her search in a room set up with bedroom furniture on loan from the old governor's mansion. Christy found no one in the room, but she did find evidence that someone had sat on the side of the bed. This incident convinced Mary Louise Prudhomme, director of the Old State Capitol, that the old building was haunted.

Freddie Deblieux's most bizarre experience occurred on the first floor: "Of all the chandeliers in the building, the one on the first floor was the only one that did not have a crown. I was standing downstairs with one of the maintenance men. He remarked how odd it was that that was the only chandelier in the building that did not have a crown that goes around the light bulbs. He ordered one, and a couple of days later, it appeared on the lamp, and it hadn't had time to come in yet."

Occasionally, little things happen in the Old State Capitol that remind staff members that they are not alone, even when they think they are. "Flashlights and ladders disappear and then show up some other place," Ms. Deblieux said. David Bonaventure, maintenance supervisor at the Old State Capitol, has had pliers and screws turn up missing, only to reappear somewhere else. Occasionally, the massive interior doors swing open and then swing closed. Ms. Deblieux credits the ghostly activity to the large number of construction projects that have gone on at the site.

Despite the unusual occurrences in the Old State Capitol, Freddie Deblieux has never been really scared there. In fact, she incorporates her weird experiences in the old building in lectures that she presents in the community. "I have spoken on the building three or four hours at a time because there is so much going on here," she said. "People never seem to get tired of hearing these old stories."

The Old State Capitol is located at 100 North Boulevard in Baton Rouge, Louisiana; phone: 225-342-0500.

Destrehan Plantation

*I*n 1994, Destrehan Plantation achieved national fame as one of the locations featured in the film *Interview with a Vampire*. Actually, though, Destrehan has been known as one of Louisiana's finest plantation homes for over two hundred years. The French-Colonial-style plantation house was built between 1787 and 1790 by Robin DeLogny, who lived there two years before his death in 1792. In 1810, the house was purchased by DeLogny's daughter, Celeste, and her husband, Jean Noel d'Estrehan. As their family grew, the d'Estrehans added twin wings. Jean died in 1823, and his wife followed him in death in 1824. Daughters of Celeste and Jean continued to live at Destrehan for many years. In 1840, Louise and Judge Pierre Rost remodeled the house to Greek Revival. In 1861, while the Rosts were on vacation in Europe, the Union army seized Destrehan and converted it into the Rost Home Colony, where newly freed slaves learned trades under the supervision of the Freedman's Bureau. The Rosts reclaimed their home in 1865. Following

Pierre's death in 1868, his widow and son lived in the plantation house. In 1910, the plantation was sold to the Destrehan Planting and Manufacturing Company. The old house passed through a series of owners. Destrehan sat abandoned for twelve years until 1971, when the River Road Historical Society was formed to preserve the home from further deterioration. Today, the magnificent plantation house has been restored to its former glory, complete with early to mid-nineteenth-century furnishings, docents dressed in period costumes, and, quite possibly, the spirits of the former inhabitants.

Destrehan Plantation has a long history of suffering and death. In 1811, twenty-one ringleaders of an uprising involving as many as two hundred slaves were tried at Destrehan and sentenced to die. Their heads were stuck on pikes along River Road as a warning to others. A series of family tragedies also contributed to Destrehan's sad legacy. One early resident, Nicholas Noel, lost his right arm when his cape became tangled in some plantation machinery. His fifteen-year-old bride died soon after their marriage. His second wife died very young in a yellow fever epidemic. His sister Zelia died mysteriously at age thirty in New York City. A brother, Rene Noel, also died of an undetermined cause at age twenty-eight.

Legends about Destrehan Plantation have circulated for a long time. In the 1960s, rumors began flying around Destrehan that the pirate Jean Lafitte had hidden booty stolen from Spanish treasure ships in the walls during one of his visits to the plantation house. Vandals ripped out several of the interior walls, but no treasure was ever found. Destrehan's ghost stories began circulating soon after the old house was restored in the 1980s. It is generally believed that the house is haunted by the ghost of Stephen Henderson, who lived here with his wife, Eleanor, in the early 1800s. The Hendersons enjoyed only one year of marital bliss before Eleanor died at age nineteen. Heartbroken, Stephen became a mere shadow of his former self, finally passing away a few years later. Visitors claim to have seen a white figure crossing the driveway, gazing out windows, and sitting in a chair. Spectral lights and disembodied faces have also been spotted by museum staff and delivery drivers. It is said that the spirit of a former owner once attended a reception at the manor. A few people have speculated that the spirit might be that of Henderson's friend, Jean Lafitte, but Henderson himself is a more likely candidate for the ghost because Destrehan was the scene of his greatest happiness and his greatest sorrow.

Not all of the ghosts at Destrehan Plantation are adults. For many years, a little blond girl between the ages of five and seven has been seen, usually in the nursery. One staff member said that he was taking a shortcut through the nursery one day when he saw a little girl playing on an antique rocking horse. Thinking that she might have wandered off from a tour, he decided to open the door. As he moved into the room, the girl jumped off the rocking horse and disappeared. Other tour guides claim that the little girl has hidden behind their wide hoop skirts as they walked into the nursery. One visitor said that he had seen two little girls playing on the staircase in the foyer. The younger child had light-colored hair, and the older one had dark hair and dark eyes.

For years, one could find convincing evidence of the presence of ghosts at Destrehan's Gift Shop. Several ghostly photographs taken by tourists were put on display. In one of the photographs, the image of a man wearing a high collar and a cape was clearly visible. The specter was floating above the staircase in the entrance foyer. Not long afterward, a psychic who had been touring the house told the cashier that she had seen a ghostly figure standing in the upstairs hall. She described him as wearing a light-green waistcoat with a high collar. The man stood motionless, apparently gazing at the wall along the back of the house. She found the direction in which the man was staring to be particularly puzzling because there was no window in that part of the wall. She was also struck by the fact that the man had no right hand.

Intrigued by the woman's story, the cashier accompanied the psychic upstairs to see the ghost for herself. The cashier did not see or hear anything, but the psychic maintained that he was still there. This time, she was able to see his face even more clearly. She said that he was a tall man with dark hair and a sharp nose. He was standing between the parlor and the nursery room doors. A few minutes later, she said that the spirit had left. One of the tour guides then showed the woman an antique photograph of Nicholas Noel Destrehan that usually sat on top of the air conditioner in the gift shop. The woman was fairly certain that the man she had seen in the upstairs hall was the same man in the old photograph.

The haunting activity in Destrehan Plantation seems to have died down in the past decade. In fact, the tour guides no longer include ghost stories as a part of their tour. One can only hope that Stephen Henderson's melancholy spirit has finally found eternal rest. Undoubtedly, his memory will live on in the ghost stories that are still passed down by people in the community.

Destrehan Plantation is thirteen miles north of New Orleans. It faces the Mississippi River. The address is 9999 River Road, Destrehan, LA 70047; phone: 985-764-8544.

St. Vincent's Guest House

NEW ORLEANS

ach year, thousands of visitors are lured to New Orleans by its abundance of historic hotels and inns. Many of these establishments were originally privately owned mansions in the nineteenth century. One of the city's most unique inns is St. Vincent's Guest House. The large, imposing building was built in 1861 as an orphanage. Over the years, reports from guests and staff at the old hotel lead one to believe that some of the nuns and the children have never left.

Although St. Vincent's Orphanage was founded by an order of nuns called the Daughters of Charity, much of the funding was provided by a philanthropist named Margaret Haughery, known locally as "the Mother of the Orphans." She was born in Cavan, Ireland, in 1814. She became an orphan in 1822 after the death of her parents in Baltimore, Maryland. She was taken in by a kind-hearted Welsh family but was never taught to read or write. In 1835, she married Charles Haughery and moved to New Orleans. Within a year, however, Charles and their infant son died of yellow fever. Four years after her husband's death, she took up work in the local Orphans' Asylum. When food supplies ran low, she replenished them with money from her own earnings. Through Margaret's financial assistance, the Orphans' Asylum was cleared of debt. During the yellow fever epidemic of 1853, Margaret went from house to house nursing the victims. After the epidemic was over, she was approached with the need of caring for infants who were now left alone. Margaret's answer was, "Build the asylum, and God will pay for it." In 1861, St. Vincent De Paul's Infant Asylum was built. Local lore has it that Margaret charmed the Union army into laying the foundation for the orphanage. The mortgage was paid off in sixteen years, largely through Margaret's milk cart sales.

Aside from being a charitable person, Margaret was also a shrewd businesswoman. She established a dairy and a bakery and delivered milk and bread herself. "Margaret's Bakery," which was the first steam bakery in the South, prospered and Margaret's fortunes increased. During the Civil War, Margaret got permission from General Benjamin Butler to carry flour for her orphans and Confederate prisoners across the lines. During her lifetime, she established four orphanages and several homes for the elderly. When she died in 1882, she left the bulk of her estate—over $600,000—to orphanages in New Orleans. Her pallbearers included former governors and mayors. A statue of her was unveiled on July 9, 1884. The little park in which it is erected is called Margaret's Place. Her statue is one of the first erected in the United States to honor a woman.

St. Vincent's operated as an orphanage for infants and young children for over one hundred years. After the children turned seven, the girls were taken from St. Vincent's to St. Elizabeth's on Napoleon Avenue. In the nineteenth century, most of the orphans came from families that had been decimated by the frequent outbreaks of yellow fever. After 1901, when it was discovered that mosquitoes were the cause of the summer epidemics, the city began paving the roads. Once the number of puddles in the city was reduced, the mosquito population declined. Without the annual epidemics, the number of orphans in the city was also reduced. St. Vincent's then operated as a home for unwed mothers until the stigma of bearing illegitimate children began to diminish in the 1960s. The babies were delivered in the middle wing. The nuns also set up a large room with rows of sinks and sewing machines where the girls learned parenting skills. In the mid-1970s, St. Vincent's closed down because it became too expensive to operate. The old building stood empty for twenty years until it reopened as St. Vincent's Guest House in 1994.

Not surprisingly, most of the ghosts in St. Vincent's Guest House are the spirits of children, some of whom died in the orphanage of yellow fever. A frequent occurrence in the Guest House is the sound of children running down the hallway and giggling behind the walls. Occasionally, though, the child ghosts make an appearance inside the rooms. Larry Sargent, a guest at St. Vincent's from May 6 to May 18, 2003, claims to have had his sleep disturbed by the ghosts: "Every night since I've been here, I've had several little tow-headed kids in bed with me. Usually, they bounce on the bed and say, 'Wake up, Uncle Larry! Come play with us!' And I say, 'Leave me alone. I'm tired.' They have bounced on the bed so hard that they've broken the box springs." His girlfriend, Lois Gordon, believes that the children are attracted to Larry because he is a very loving man: "Larry has no children of his own. He's just had several close relatives die, and I guess the little orphans sense that he needs somebody to love." Sargent has become so attached to the children that he does not even think of them as being ghosts. "I think they just want someone to pay attention to them," he said.

Ulysses Morrero, a former desk clerk at St. Vincent's, recalled a terrifying encounter a fellow employee had with the ghost children while living in the attic: "He had two dogs. He couldn't keep them up in the attic because they'd have their tails between their legs. They'd whimper. The first chance they got, they'd run outside. One night, he heard the main door in the second wing slam shut. Then he heard footsteps coming up the steps, and he panicked. He hid in one of the cabinets and spent a good part of the night there. He was chilled to the bone." Thinking that the ghosts were gone, the man climbed out of the cabinet and returned to bed. He had not been asleep for more than an hour before the noises started up again: "He was awakened several times by the sound of children running around the bed. At one point, he felt the covers being pulled off him. He came down to the front desk and told me, 'I can't stay here!'" Morrero found the man's story to be credible because he was Swiss, whom Morrero described as "very logical people." Afterward, Morrero found out that children who had misbehaved were locked in the attic and forced to kneel and do penance in the same spot where Confederate prisoners had been chained during the Civil War.

Morrero had a personal meeting with the Guest House's mischievous spirits one night while he was working the front desk: "I had heard some of the other employees say that sometimes the lights in the lobby would grow dim after a while. I found this hard to believe because the dimming switch was in a locked hallway. One night when I started work, I went into the hallway, turned on the lights in the lobby, left the room, and locked the door. After a little while, the lights began to dim. I know it wasn't an electrical problem because I went back to the locked hallway, and the knob had been turned [to dim]."

The ghostly figure of a nun has also been seen in St. Vincent's Guest House. Peter Schreiber, the owner of St. Vincent's, says that at least three guests have told him about the nun: "Some people have seen a white figure walking down the stairway. She's always been seen in the middle wing. That wing had only been partially renovated. Some of the old very sad writing about life here was still on the wall. Some of the old cribs were here too. They looked like cages. I imagine it was a pretty tough life here. The nuns really made the kids tow the line." According to Ulysses Morrero, a maid from Sweden also saw the nun in the middle wing. The nun was looking at her from the balcony. The maid quit shortly thereafter. He said that several guests saw the nun: "The next morning, they would tell us, 'We didn't know you still had nuns on the property.' I'd say, 'There's one still left' because I didn't want to scare the guests."

The paranormal activity at St. Vincent's Guest House bears all the characteristics of a residual haunting, which author Tom Ogden defines as "people and events made up of psychic energy that is somehow imprinted on a location" (Ogden 1999, 206). At various times, the event discharges and plays back, just as a recording would. Ulysses Morrero also believes that this explanation, which he first heard from a psychic guest, applies to what is going on at St. Vincent's: "I know these sightings are real because several people have told me the same stories without having talked to each other. A guest at St. Vincent's said that the reason why everyone hears the same thing is because it's a residual haunting." One would like to think that the children continue to run and play at St. Vincent's Guest House because this is the only home they have ever known.

St. Vincent's Guest House is located at 1507 Magazine Street, New Orleans, LA 70130; phone: 866-282-9330.

Mississippi

Merrehope

Merrehope is a resilient gem, a survivor of war, time, and progress. This antebellum mansion in Meridian, Mississippi, was originally a simple cottage. It was built in 1858 by the city's earliest settler, Richard McLemore, for his daughter, Juriah Jackson. In 1864, the cottage was used as headquarters for Confederate general Leonidas Polk. Following Polk's exit from Meridian, the cottage was occupied by several of General William Tecumseh Sherman's officers. It was one of fewer than six buildings left standing after General Sherman's Valentine's Day visit of 1864. The home was expanded after the war by the John Gary family. The final renovation of Merrehope was completed by the S. H. Floyd family in 1904. Merrehope was divided into eight apartments in the 1930s, and it continued to operate as a boardinghouse into the 1960s. Merrehope was purchased by the Meridian Restorations Foundation in 1968 and restored. The elegant old mansion now serves as a showplace for local social functions. For over thirty-five years,

Merrehope has served as a sort of portal to the past, especially for the hostesses and guests who have encountered its ghostly residents.

Fonda Rush, Meridian's former historical preservationist and current director of the local chapter of Habitat for Humanity, has been involved with the house since the foundation first bought it. In 1973 during her last year in college, Fonda had just begun working as a hostess at Merrehope when she decided to show the house to her boyfriend. She walked up on the side porch, and he walked onto the front porch. Both of them saw a female figure standing in the center of the room, looking at them. She was wearing an 1870's period hoop skirt. They both ran back down the stairs to the car and drove off. A few days later, one of the ladies on the board showed Fonda a couple of portraits of Eugenia and Pristina Gary, the daughters of John Gary, that the foundation had just acquired from the Gary family. Both young women had died of consumption at the end of the Civil War and were buried in Alabama. An uneasy feeling crept over Fonda as she recognized Eugenia as the young woman she had seen standing in the front room.

Fonda's daughter also had an encounter with Eugenia. One October night during a Halloween party, Fonda and her daughter were wearing period clothing as they greeted their guests. Her daughter was standing on the balcony outside the Museum Room where Eugenia's portrait hangs when she felt as if someone were watching her. She turned around and saw Eugenia standing in the window. At that moment, "getting into the Halloween spirit" assumed an entirely different meaning for her.

Visitors of all types have also sensed that Merrehope is haunted. During one of Fonda's tours, two ladies came up to her and said, "You have a ghost in Merrehope, don't you?" When Fonda asked how they knew, one of them replied that they had heard her singing in the bathroom connected to the Bride's Room. Eugenia also turns the lights back on as the hostesses walk to their cars at night, and she even plays the piano. According to Fonda, Eugenia apparently set off one of the motion detectors one night. She also seems to have frightened off a couple of burglars who broke a window and entered the apartment in the basement but apparently left in a great hurry before they could steal anything. A few months later, the wife of one of the carpenters was walking outside of the house in search of her husband when she saw a woman staring out the window. The carpenter said that he was alone the entire afternoon. During one summer when the air conditioning on the second floor was cut off, guests experienced an eerie cold sensation while standing in front of Eugenia's portrait in the Museum Room.

Rush believes that there is a second spirit in the house. Back in the 1940s, a former teacher who was renting the Periwinkle Room on the second floor became very despondent while drinking late one night. After one of his poker parties, he placed several whiskey bottles on the mantle in his room and loaded his pistol. He shot each of the bottles and then shot himself in the head. One can still see places in the mantle where the bullet holes have been filled up. Unlike Eugenia, the ghost of the suicidal teacher never leaves his room. Over the years, hostesses and guests have smelled cigar smoke and experienced cold spots in the Periwinkle Room.

Occasionally, spirits attempt to enter the house from the outside. For example, on a stormy afternoon in March 2003, Rush was showing a young couple around the house in preparation for their wedding reception. She had work to do upstairs, so she told the bride-to-be to just yell if she needed anything. After a half hour, Fonda heard the door bell. "It wasn't just a ding," Fonda said. "It was a frantic ring, like someone was pressing down really hard on the buzzer." As Fonda walked down the stairs, she saw the vague outline of a man through the rose-tinted glass on the door. When she opened the door, there was no one there. "I'm sure it was one of those Union soldiers trying to get in," Fonda explained. "They have tried do it before." Disc jockey Scotty Ray Boyd also made the acquaintance of the mansion's ghostly visitor during one of radio station WOKK's three Halloween visits: "The first time we were there, Debbie Alexander [Boyd's co-host] and I were the only ones remaining in the house on Halloween morning. It was about 8:50, and I heard the footsteps on the front porch. Then the doorbell rang. I went to the door, and there was no one there. There was no way somebody could have left without us hearing the footsteps walk off the porch."

Footsteps have been heard inside the house after hours as well. A renter who lives in a basement apartment says that he has heard people walking around the house late at night several times. Boyd heard the spectral footsteps on his first visit to Merrehope: "While we were eating in the kitchen, we could hear faint footsteps right above our heads. It sounded like someone was walking in the middle of the second-floor hallway."

Fonda speculates that Eugenia's ghost might have come to Merrehope with her portrait. The portraits were originally in the possession of the Gary family, who had moved to the Mississippi Gulf Coast shortly after John Gary's death. In 1969, the portraits were damaged by Hurricane Camille. Soon after the Gary family gave the portraits to Merrehope, they were sent to the Mississippi University for Women to have one of their professors look at restoring them. During the seven-month period while the portraits were being examined, all of the haunting activity in the old house ceased. The ghostly phenomena resumed almost immediately after the portraits were returned.

The haunting activity at Merrehope has shown no signs of abating. In fact, unexplained occurrences are still being reported by the old mansion's current hostesses. Donna White, who is distantly related to the Gary family, began working as a hostess in the fall of 2002. Two weeks after starting her new job, Donna realized that Merrehope was not just another old house: "I had just checked out all the rooms, and everything was in fine shape. I came in the next morning, I walked around the house to make sure everything was O.K. When I went into the Periwinkle Room, I discovered the impression where someone had slept in the bed. I had straightened out the bed before I left the day before, so I knew that something weird had happened. I left that room in a hurry. I didn't check to see if the bed was warm or not. I went back later in the day and made the bed. The same thing has happened two other times. I'm just used to it now. It doesn't bother me like it did that first day. Several other hostesses have had the same thing happen to them." Soon afterward, Donna received her first clue that the strange things also happen in the Museum Room: "One other time, I was standing in the hall outside of Eugenia's room on the second floor, and the door to the bookcase in the hallway opened by itself."

Eerie crashing noises, like those heard at other Mississippi antebellum mansions like Waverly in West Point and Springfield Plantation in rural Jefferson County, have also been heard at Merrehope in recent years. Donna White heard the crashing sound in December 2002 when she was preparing for a Christmas party that was to be held in Merrehope: "I was here with the caterers before the people came. I was standing right by the kitchen door. Two of the ladies had just brought food in and placed it on the table when we all heard a horrible crash upstairs. I ran upstairs, and I expected to see broken glass all over the floor, but everything was just fine. I then said out loud [to the ghosts], 'There's no need for you to get so upset. We're just having a little fun downstairs.' I called Will and told her about it, and she said, 'Yeah, somebody else heard it before too.' I heard it again this past Thursday [January 23, 2003]. I was all by myself this time. Back in December, though, there were three of us downstairs in the kitchen, and we all heard it. Stuff like that makes it interesting. There's never a dull moment around here."

Longtime board member and fund-raiser Anne McKee is very familiar with Merrehope's uncanny occurrences. Although she has never experienced anything out of the ordinary herself in the old house, she has been in close contact with people who have. Anne recalls a particularly unnerving incident that took place during the 1998 Christmas season. On this particular day, eight honors students from West Lauderdale High School were invited to assist with decorating the Christmas trees that were placed in all the rooms. One boy in particular stood out from his classmates. "He was with the group, but he was somewhat segregated. He was tall and lanky and very slender, somewhat underweight. He was light complected and had long dark hair. As I was checking the names off, he confided to me that he loved Merrehope but could never get his parents to drive him there." McKee was so taken with the young man's enthusiasm that she suggested that he choose one of the trees in the upstairs rooms and decorate it himself. "I took him upstairs, and he went to the Museum Room. About an hour later, he came back. I thought he was white before, but this time, he was ashen. He said, 'I'm not going back there.' I said, 'Why?' He said, 'Because I saw something.' I said, 'What did you see?' He said, 'I saw her. She was standing at the window and was looking out.' I said, 'What room was she in?' He said, 'The Museum Room. She had on a long white dress, and she's got long dark hair, and she has really white skin.' " One of the hostesses named Wanda Clay asked the young man to take her upstairs so she could see the ghost for herself: "So Wanda walked with him to the end of the hall, and they stood in the doorway of the Museum Room, and Wanda said, 'Where is she?' And he said, 'Right there.' And she said, 'Where?' And he pointed and said, 'Oh, she just looked over at us.' Wanda said she didn't see anything, but I feel like the boy did see something."

Anne had another meeting with a "sensitive" visitor to Merrehope in November 2002 when a young woman who had recently moved to Meridian from Texas expressed an interest in visiting Merrehope. When the young woman arrived, a tour was just getting underway, so she and Anne joined the hostess and two other guests: "As we were going up the main stairway, she said, 'There's something going on here.' She glanced down the central hall and looked over toward the Museum Room. Once again, she said, 'There's something going on over here.' So we walked down the central hall, and as soon as she stepped into the Museum Room, she saw the dress on the mannequin move. She said, 'I don't feel comfortable with this.' She didn't say much; then she nodded over across the hall and said, 'There's something else going on over there.' I let her lead the way. We went into the bedroom directly across the hall through the sitting room, and she said, 'I believe there's something in this part of the house.' So we walked into the suicide room, and I told her what had happened here, and she said, 'Um hum. I don't like this feeling.' After the tour was over, the young woman told Anne that she has felt the presence of spectral beings before. 'It happens all the time. I just sense it.'"

On October 30, 2002, the first scientific investigation of Merrehope took place during an all-night stay at the old mansion. The visit was sponsored by radio station WOKK. Donovan Murphy, a ghost hunter from Birmingham, Alabama, walked through the house with an electromagnetic field meter, but he did not pick up any significant readings anywhere except for the lower portion of the main stairway inside the house. Murphy, accompanied by a local fireman, decided to check the accuracy of his findings by looking for power sources in the cellar. The men found a power line that appeared to run under the stairs. From Murphy's point of view, this discovery negated the significance of the EMF meter readings on the stairs. The Polaroid photographs he took in every room in the house also failed to reveal the presence of ghosts.

Murphy's skepticism rapidly diminished after the disc jockeys and the guests retired for the night. Between 2:00 and 4:30 A.M., he heard strange sounds in rooms where nobody was present: "Throughout the night, I heard all sorts of bumping and thumping upstairs. I seem to recall that after everyone settled down at two o'clock, it seemed really 'bumpy' upstairs until four. It sounded like somebody knocking on stuff upstairs in the Periwinkle Room. I also heard somebody walking around toward the gift shop area. A couple of times, it sounded like something came around that way towards the bathroom. I checked out everybody who was asleep, and nobody appeared to have gone to the bathroom." At 2:30, Murphy grabbed his camera and ran upstairs to the Periwinkle Room to investigate some weird noises, but by the time he reached the top of the stairs, the sounds had stopped.

Murphy's strangest experience in Merrehope occurred in the Museum Room: "I went upstairs to Eugenia's room to reset the camera, and the curio cabinet door just popped open. I came running back downstairs. That was a little bit unnerving. This makes me think there's something going on in that room."

The four teachers from Patrician Academy who were invited to spend the night at Merrehope had had a strange experience in the Museum Room several months before their Halloween visit. During Christmas break,

Linda Couch, Lolane Lewis, Sheela McBride, and Pam Hearst drove over to Meridian for a day's shopping and stopped off at Merrehope for a tour. While they were upstairs in the Museum Room listening to stories about Eugenia and her sister, the closet door opened by itself. The tour guide shut the door and opened it again with great difficulty because the wooden door had swollen and did not fit into the frame very well. Convinced that some other force must have opened the door, the tour guide suggested that the ladies go into one of the other rooms because Eugenia did not appear to want them in her room. While they were looking at the antiques in an adjoining room, the doorbell rang, and the tour guide went downstairs to answer it. When she returned upstairs, she told the ladies that no one was at the door. She interpreted this phenomenon as a sign that Eugenia did not want them upstairs at all, so the group proceeded downstairs. Nothing unusual occurred during the remainder of their tour.

Ironically, the most potentially paranormal event took place while Murphy was in the kitchen changing the film in his camera. At midnight, four of the guests from Patrician Academy were sitting in the parlor with me watching the computer monitor receiving images from the Museum Room. At 12:35 A.M., all of us saw the door to the curio cabinet in the Museum Room open and close by itself. I immediately ran upstairs, thinking that maybe someone was playing a trick. When I entered the

Museum Room, I found no one there. I then searched all of the other rooms on the second floor but found nothing. Afterward, I mentioned the incident with the curio cabinet to one of the hostesses at Merrehope. She told me that other people had seen the door open by itself before, but no one had ever seen it close. I still cannot explain the curio cabinet's uncanny behavior that night. Disc jockey Scotty Ray Boyd was equally befuddled: "If you heard somebody say that the door opened by itself, you'd think they were crazy. But I saw it happen on the video camera when nothing else was in the room. You might be able to explain the door opening by itself due to the house shifting or maybe an unlevel floor, but it wouldn't close up and latch up by itself."

So far, the permanent residents of Merrehope have shown no interest in "crossing over to the other side." To many of the mansion's more psychic visitors, Eugenia, the "nice" ghost, is a protective spirit who appreciates the efforts of the Meridian Restorations Foundation and of the Friends of Merrehope to save it for future generations to enjoy. On the other hand, the cantankerous spirit in the Periwinkle Room seems to relish his role as a "scary" ghost. Like many men, though, he does not seem to enjoy making the bed.

Merrehope is located at 905 Martin Luther King Jr. Memorial Drive; phone: 601-483-8439.

Corinth Battlefield

uring the Civil War, Corinth, Mississippi, was very important from a military viewpoint. The east-west Memphis and Charleston Railroad and the north-south Mobile and Ohio Railroad intersected here. These railroads linked Virginia with Memphis, Mobile, and Columbus, Kentucky. In 1862, Corinth could have served as an offensive springboard into Tennessee and Kentucky. The loss of Corinth would force the evacuation of Memphis and much of northern Mississippi and northwestern Alabama. In the spring of 1862, General P. G. T. Beauregard prepared for the defense of the town. Entrenchments covering the northern and eastern approaches to Corinth were extended to an arc about one and one-half miles from town.

On April 29, Union troops under the command of Major General Henry W. Halleck and General Ulysses S. Grant began the advance on Corinth. By early May, the siege of Corinth began. Beauregard tried to cut off and destroy a portion of the Union army, but by May 9, he had decided that Corinth was untenable. On the night of May 29, Beauregard's army successfully withdrew to the Tupelo area. The Union armies occupied Corinth on the morning of May 30.

Confederate forces under the command of General Braxton Bragg planned to retake Corinth in early October. Before General Halleck left for Washington, he had ordered that a defensive line be constructed to protect Corinth from the west or the south. When General William Rosencrans positioned his 23,000 troops in and around Corinth on October 2, his line was much shorter than Beauregard's line had been the spring before. A line of batteries was connected by breastworks strengthened by logs sharpened and arranged in front for greater defense.

Confederate forces began their attack on Corinth on October 3 at about ten o'clock in the morning. Rosencrans stationed three divisions into the old Confederate rifle pits north and northwest of town. The fourth division was held in reserve south of town. By evening, the Confederates had forced the Union soldiers south two miles, back into the inner line of fortifications. During the night, Rosencrans positioned his troops in an arch-shaped line two miles long. The next morning, the Confederates stormed Battery Powell, but Union counterattacks soon drove them from the town. By noon the Confederates had retreated toward the northwest. The Confederates had lost 4,800 of their 22,000

men. The Federals had lost 2,350 of their 23,000 soldiers. The Union army continued to occupy Corinth
until the winter of 1863-64.

The conflict that scarred the city forever is recreated
periodically by Civil War reenactors, most of whom
attempt to live in the same conditions endured by their
ancestors over a century before. One of these reenactors,
Bonnie Hallman from Huntsville, Alabama, had two very
unsettling experiences in her tent one Friday night in a
very crowded camping area: "I went to bed a little early.
Everybody else was still up. There were still people standing around my tent talking. I hadn't been in bed for very
long before I heard all these cavalry horses come racing
behind my tent. I was so angry because they were gallop-
ing hell for leather. I was so mad. I jumped up and ran
outside the tent. There was a bunch of people standing
out there, and I wasn't using the nicest language in the
world. But the question was, 'Who the devil were those
people who rode behind my tent?' They said, 'Who?' I
said, 'The cavalry who came racing behind my tent. They
could have killed somebody riding through camp like
that.' 'There wasn't anybody riding through camp,' they
said. I was the only one who heard it."

Bonnie Hallman had an even closer encounter with
the supernatural a few nights later. It had rained the
night before, and she and her husband had laid down
straw on the ground before pitching their tent. They
were camped in almost the exact spot where Grant's

troops had been: "It was late at night. We had tied our tent flaps together and gone to bed. My husband was asleep in his cot. All of a sudden, I heard him walking around in the straw. I lay there thinking, 'If I let him know I'm awake, he's going to want me to help him look for whatever he's looking for.' He continued walking around and lifting the lids off boxes. And then, all of a sudden, I heard my husband snoring. He was not the one walking around the tent. I thought, 'Maybe some idiot is in here robbing us.' I lay there absolutely terrified. I finally got up and looked around, and there was nobody there. I got a tennis shoe and threw it at my husband because I was too scared to move. He woke up and said, 'What is it?' and I said, 'Somebody has been in this tent walking around.' He said, 'I heard that a while ago, but I thought it was you.' I said, 'No, I've been lying here listening to that noise.' He said, 'Well, maybe there really is somebody else in the tent.' So he got up and checked the flaps, and they were still tightly closed. There is no way a grown person could have crawled under the flaps. Even a child would have had difficulty getting in."

Like many nineteenth-century railroad centers, Corinth's prominence has declined over the years. As trains gave way to automobiles as the primary modes of transportation in the twentieth century, towns like Corinth have become more important for their historical significance. The siege of Corinth has left an indelible impression on the town and on the South in general.

Paranormal incidents like those experienced by Bonnie Hallman and others in Corinth are reminders that, in the South, the past has not really passed.

Corinth Battlefield is in Corinth, Mississippi, on U.S. routes 45 and 72, eight miles south of the Tennessee border. Five acres of the historic battlefield are within the boundaries of Fort Robinette at the intersection of Wenasoga Road and Linden Street.

The Old Cahill Mansion

HANDSBORO

S ome houses live on in local lore long after the structures themselves are gone. A good example of such a house is the legendary Cahill Mansion in Handsboro, Mississippi. Constructed in 1915 by William Stewart on a site overlooking Bayou Bernard, the elegant three-story mansion was the pride of Handsboro. Like many grand old houses, the Cahill Mansion eventually fell upon hard times. During World War II, the house was used as an NCO club. Before long, the house was known as a "wild" place, frequented by gamblers and prostitutes. After the war, the Cahill Mansion once again became a private residence. During this time, the Cahill Mansion acquired an entirely different reputation as the most haunted house on the Gulf Coast.

A former resident of Handsboro, Anne Milstead, is well acquainted with the ghosts in the Cahill Mansion. "We went to church with Dr. and Mrs. Gregory, who bought the house in 1957," Milstead said. "One night back in 1972, Mrs. Gregory came to our youth group and told stories about the old house." One of Mrs. Gregory's stories focused on the Cahill family, who lived in the house in the 1950s. In 1953, their thirteen-year-old son was killed in a tractor accident on the property. According to Anne Milstead, the ghost of the Cahill boy was one of the spirits haunting the mansion: "A lot of people saw him hanging around the kitchen. Mrs. Gregory had a friend over one day when Mr. Gregory was out of town. Well, he called, and Mrs. Gregory told him that her friend had left the room so they could talk privately. When Mrs. Gregory's friend went in to the kitchen, there was a little boy standing there talking on the phone. They had a bunch of children, and she said, 'Put that down' to give the Gregorys some privacy, and the little boy disappeared. So later when she was telling Mrs. Gregory about the young man, Mrs. Gregory said, 'Would you mind looking at some pictures?' When the lady was going through the pictures, she said, 'That's him! Right here!' Mrs. Gregory said, 'Are you sure that's who you saw?' And the lady said, 'Well, yes. He had blond hair.' Mrs. Gregory said, 'That's the Cahill boy, and he's been dead for twenty years!' They saw him several times."

Mrs. Gregory's five-year-old son was the first member of her family to have contact with the ghosts in the house. One night, shortly after they moved into the house, he went into his mother's bedroom and told her that someone was walking around his room at night. They told him that he was imagining things and sent him back to bed. Later that night, the little boy woke up his mother again with the same complaint, so she sent an older brother to stay with him. About an hour later, the older boy ran into his mother's bedroom and said, "He's not lying. There's someone walking around at night. The closet door opened up, and the footsteps would go around the bed and go back to the closet."

On November 17, 1963, the little boy once again became the target of the ghosts in the house. Mrs. Gregory said her son walked into his bedroom, and his school jacket lying across the bed suddenly burst into flames. Hearing the screams of the child, the maid ran downstairs to the little boy's room. By the time she put out the flames, the jacket had already been partially destroyed. Incidents such as this one made it difficult for the Gregorys to keep maids.

During the twelve years that the Gregory family lived in the Cahill Mansion, a series of weird occurrences supported Mrs. Gregory's initial impression that they were not alone in the house. She said that some days, the strange sounds in the house, like grating noises and screams, would become so loud that she would have to wear earplugs. She also reported feeling very cold in some of the rooms of the house. Strange problems with the house began to surface, such as falling light fixtures and unpaintable walls. One night, soon after she and her family moved into the house, a group of college boys, including her son, were awakened in the middle of the night by what sounded like footsteps running through their room. On the day of President John F. Kennedy's assassination, the family woke to find blood dripping down the draperies and smeared on the windows. According to Anne Milstead, though, Mrs. Gregory never really felt threatened by the spirits except for the night when she and her husband were in their bedroom and were startled by a loud noise, almost as if someone had struck the headboard with his fist. Anne still recalls how Mrs. Gregory described the sound to her youth group: "When Mrs. Gregory was talking about the ghost hitting the headboard, she hit a table—'Bam!'—to show how loud it was, and everyone in our youth group jumped."

The Gregorys finally moved out of the house in the late 1960s because the upkeep was more than they could handle. The Gregorys had originally planned to have the old house razed, but they were unable to arrange it after Hurricane Camille struck the coast because contractors were tied up clearing away debris. After Hurricane Camille, several windows in the home were boarded up, and rain warped the flooring on the third level as a result of roof damage. For several months while the house stood vacant, curiosity seekers flocked to the house, lured by the stories that had been circulating for over a decade. Some of Anne Milstead's high school friends were among those hardier souls who dared to spend the night in the decrepit old mansion: "After Camille, groups of kids would go there, and usually one of the Gregorys' kids was with them. Nothing would happen to them if one of the Gregorys was there. They said that the toaster would fly through the air and the coffee pot would do this and that." The Gregorys estimated that in the year their home stood vacant, vandals caused $39,000 worth of damages.

Toward the end, the Gregorys opened their house to ghost hunters and clairvoyants. One of these researchers was a Tennessee minister named Dr. David Bubar, who was nationally recognized for his ability to talk to spirits. In 1969, during a psychic investigation attended by about twenty people, Dr. Bubar went into a self-imposed trance and made contact with the resident spirits. Several spirits, through Bubar's voice, claimed to have died violently during those years when the Cahill Mansion was used as an NCO Club. One of these ghosts was a young woman named Flossie, who, through Dr. Bubar, told a tale of forced prostitution, abortion, and her own murder: "I am Flossie, and I'm hurt. My nose, my head, my neck doesn't even work anymore . . . He wanted to use me. He keeps me in this room and locks the door . . . My baby. I wanted to keep my baby . . . He shot me. I'm sick. I'm corroded. I'm full of holes." Before Flossie's voice dissipated, she said that she had tried to burn down the house previously by placing lighted candles in a cabinet. Before Bubar came out of his trance, he predicted that the house would indeed be destroyed by flames so that Flossie's spirit and all of the other ghosts in the house would find release. Seven months later on July 18, 1970, at 1:20 P.M., the Cahill Mansion caught fire, just as Bubar had predicted. Ironically, a séance had been held in the old house the night before.

No trace of the old Cahill Mansion remains. The property on which the house once stood has been subdivided and now blends in with the rest of the up-scale neighborhood. Still, some people, like Anne Milstead, were sorry to see the dilapidated old house go. "There are some new homes there now. I'd be curious to know if anything has happened in those new houses. It would be nice to think that the ghosts are not gone entirely."

The Noxubee County Library

*t*he Noxubee County Library in Macon, Mississippi, is, without a doubt, one of the most colorful libraries in the entire nation. Designed by the Hull Brothers of Jackson, Mississippi, in the Romanesque style of architecture, the building served as the Noxubee County Jail from 1907 to 1977. During the 1930s, the first floor of the building was renovated to allow for living quarters for the jailers and their families. The second and third floors continued to be used as holding cells. The building ceased to be used as a county jail in 1977, and it stood vacant until 1983 when the library board began renovating the building with a $106,000 grant. The library was officially rededicated on February 3, 1985. Iron bars on the second- and third-floor windows are still plainly visible from the street. The metal doors from the three jail cells on the third floor remain as well. The kitchen and the restroom on the second floor were originally the women's jail cells. The director's office and the "mechanical" room where the air-conditioning unit is stored were the men's jail cells. The Youth Fiction and Adult Biography section on the third floor originally had an inner and outer cell. The dangerous criminals were kept in the inner cell, and the drunks were placed in the outer cell. Some of the bars from these cells are still in place. The library also has one of only two working gallows in the state of Mississippi. The bodies would have fallen through a trap door and hang suspended in the air on the second floor as an object lesson to all of the prisoners within viewing distance. At one time, the hangman's rope was still in place, but the librarians removed it to prevent children from accidentally hanging themselves. The gallows was never used because hanging was outlawed in Mississippi after the execution of a black man named Si Connor, one of the library's resident ghosts.

The story of Si Connor's arrest, incarceration, and execution were published in the September 28, 1907, edition of the *Macon Beacon*. After finding out that his wife was having an affair with a man named Jake, Si told her she would have to choose which man she wanted to spend the rest of her life with. His wife refused, so one day, he sneaked behind her in a cotton patch and nearly cut her head off with a knife. Without bothering to clean himself up, Si walked into town and announced that he had just killed his wife. At first, the townspeople thought he had gone insane. A few of the more curious spectators went out to Si's farm to check out his story and discovered the bloody corpse of his wife, still lying in the field.

Si was arrested a few hours later and taken to a cell in the Noxubee County Jail. After he was found guilty of his wife's murder, Si was ordered to be hanged in the jail, but he asked for a public hanging instead. In an interview with a local reporter shortly before his execution, Si claimed that the spirits of his wife and her lover were in his jail cell and had been ever since he was arrested. Even Jesus made an appearance: "Jesus have been here since I been in jail and have taken me to hell and showed me everything there and what sort it is." Si said that he and Jesus passed through the bars of his cell and went down to a place Si described as being "as big as Macon, maybe bigger." He saw people in a "big fire" crying for cool water. The buckets that were handed to them contained not water, but something resembling "bluein." Jesus then took Si down a narrow road to a "great big ocean of water, and I walked right up on the bank and on across this water without touching it. Then we come back across the ocean of water again and right back to jail, and here I is." Jesus also took Si out to the courthouse yard where the gallows stood. After Si walked up the thirteen steps to the trap door, Jesus forgave his sins. "And then the man like Mr. Dantzler [the sheriff] began to tie the rope around my neck and when he got it tied, two angels come down from heaven, and when he stooped to touch off the trigger after he had done drawed the black cap I had on down over my ears down to my chest, they tuck and grabbed me and took me to heaven."

Si Connor's hanging was scheduled for September 27, 1907. At 3:48, Sheriff Dantzler and Deputy Clark walked with their prisoner from the jail to the gallows. According to the article that appeared the next day in the *Macon Beacon*, Si was dressed in black "with a spot of white for a shirt front and a streak of light brown where his hair was parted." The seven or eight hundred people in the crowd, mostly from the black community, were impressed with Si's courage: "He walked with no weakening of the knees to the scaffold and up the steep steps, and when he spoke, there was no tremor or quaver in his voice; it was firm and strong and could be heard across the yard and the farther street." After a few hysterical screams from some of the women, the crowd stood in silence as the noose was placed around his neck and the hangman pulled the lever. After four minutes, Si was dead. The newspaper account of the hanging concludes with the reporter's description of the crowd's reaction: "There were curious ejaculations as to the impassiveness of the victim, there were expressions of wonder at the nerve he exhibited in the face of horrible death, and there were—from the emotional members of his own race—exclamations of admiration for his courage and his religious faith." However, if the testimony of Si's fellow prisoners can be believed, this was not Si's final appearance. For several days following Si's execution, he was seen walking down the corridors of the jail. It is said that Si still spends his nights in the jail cells, but no one recently has spent the night to determine if this story is true.

At the time of this printing, the Noxubee County Library was being given a fresh coat of paint and new carpeting. All of the jail paraphernalia, though, will remain because the building has been designated as a historical landmark. Even though Si did not die on the library's gallows, it stands as a grim reminder of the fate of a man who murdered out of love. One wonders if Si's spirit really did make the journey Jesus had shown him, or if he continues to hover around the remnants of the old jail cells.

The address for the Noxubee County Library is 103 East King Street, Macon, MS 39341; phone: 662-726-5461.

Brikalo

LAUDERDALE

*I*n frontier Mississippi, stagecoach stops were vital links between settlements. At the very least, passengers could expect to find a place to sleep, possibly some sort of wild game for supper, and a generous helping of southern hospitality. At a time when the majority of homes in Lauderdale County were log cabins, some stagecoach stops offered a touch of elegance in an untamed land. Just north of Lauderdale stands Brikalo, the country's only remaining antebellum stagecoach stop. It is located on Whiskey Road, which went from Gainseville, Alabama, to Philadelphia, Mississippi. In 1834, Vincent Delk commissioned Joseph P. Warren to build the antebellum stagecoach stop. Constructed of heart pine and slave-made bricks, Brikalo has had only four owners in its 180-year history. In 1973, the old home was lovingly restored by its present owners, Harriet and Chat McGonagill. Harriet believes that at least one of the former occupants of the old inn has made a very prolonged stay there.

In spite of the stories the McGonagills had heard about the old house, they were still shocked to learn—firsthand—that they might be sharing their new home with ghosts. The first family members who spent a night on the property were Grandmother and Grandfather McGonagill. Daunted by the prospect of sleeping in a house that had stood abandoned for twenty years, they slept in a camper. The next morning, Grandfather McGonagill said that he saw a young woman with long blonde hair waving to him from an upstairs window. Although he spent several additional nights on the premises, he refused to go inside the house. Harriet and Chat McGonagill also had an unsettling experience in their first night in the house. After they crawled into their sleeping bags, Harriet found she was unable to sleep because of the security light shining from outside the window. Her husband told her, "It's too much trouble to set a pole and move the security light. After we move in and install the drapes and blinds, you won't care how close the security light is." Dismayed by Chatt's reluctance to do anything about the light, Harriet replied, "All right, but for tonight, I just wish the light were off." Immediately, the light went off, and the house was plunged in darkness. Thinking that someone had thrown a circuit breaker, Harriet grabbed a flashlight and began shining it outside the window. Chatt told her that shining the flashlight outside the window would not help the situation. Besides, the electricity had to be on because the children were watching television downstairs. Disgusted, Harriet said, "Well, I don't care. I just wish the thing would come back on." As soon as she said that, the light came back on.

Two similar incidents occurred a few weeks later. Once, before they had installed their air-conditioning unit, Harriet and her daughters were sitting at a table in the room that is now their kitchen. It was a very warm day, so the windows were open. The windows had no screens at this time, so a number of bugs flew into the house. Frustrated by their unwelcome visitors, one of Harriet's daughters announced that she could take the heat better than the bugs, and she wished the windows were closed. "At that," Harriet said, "one widow slammed, and after about three seconds, the other window slammed." The second strange incident took place after the air conditioning was in place. The McGonagills invited a neighbor to spend the night with their daughters after returning from the rodeo. While sitting in the front parlor, Harriet's neighbor remarked, "It is surely warm in here." Harriet replied, "We'll just close the doors and turn on the air conditioning." Her friend said, "Well, I just wish that door was closed." She had just finished her statement when the door slammed shut by itself. Harriet's neighbor gathered up her things and went home. She never spent another night in the house.

The strange occurrences at Brikalo prompted Harriet to investigate some of the legends she had heard about her home. According to one story she had been told by the previous owner, Mr. Hatcher, General Sherman's troops threw torches onto the roof and rode off. The women and slaves formed a bucket brigade and put out the fire. The McGonagills had dismissed the tale as nothing more than an old legend until they removed the tin roof and found a burned circle ten feet in diameter. "The fire burned through the shingles, through the lathes, and into the logs. The logs are more than six inches thick, so structurally, the fire did not do any serious damage," Harriet said. "But it's obviously been burned. I'm glad they saved it." Mr. Hatcher also told Harriet that back in the nineteenth century, a little girl, four or five years old, was playing on a stairwell near an upstairs bedroom. While reaching for a kitten inside the banister, she fell off the stairwell and was killed. Harriet said that a five-year-old girl is indeed buried in the family plot just behind Brikalo. However, the little girl is not the only person who died in the antebellum home. Harriet said that a young man was accidentally shot to death in the front room. "The hole from the shotgun blast still remains in the ceiling," she said. After Mr. and Mrs. Delks died in 1855 and 1856, Brikalo was auctioned off and sold to Dr. Silliman, who practiced medicine there from 1869 to 1904. "Naturally," Harriet said, "there have been many deaths within the old house. Many of these were probably patients of Dr. Silliman."

One of the ghosts reputed to haunt Brikalo might well be the spirit of the little girl who fell off the stairwell. One night, Chat saw a little girl, wrapped in an Indian blanket, sitting in the darkness at the foot of the stairs. Thinking that this was his daughter, who was upset because guests had taken her bedroom, he said, "Lori, is that you?" The little girl did not respond, so Chatt turned on the light. She was gone.

Bizarre occurrences continued well into the 1980s. Late one night, as Harriet and her husband sat in the living room, their gaze was directed toward their porch swing, which could be seen through the window. Suddenly, the swing began moving by itself. Later, Harriet recalled that no breeze was blowing, and no animals were in the vicinity. Another time, while Chatt was away on a cross-country flight, Harriet noticed that he had not set the time for the old wind-up pendulum clock in one of the downstairs rooms. The next morning, not only was the clock running, but it had also been set correctly. Chatt was the only member of the household who knew how to wind and set the clock.

Harriet McGonagill admits that initially she was more interested in the history of Brikalo than in the possibility that it might be haunted. In fact, she did not want her house to have the reputation of being haunted. "When I moved here," Harriet said, "it was like coming home. I have never been afraid. So many wonderful things happened here. We consider them to be friendly spirits."

Brikalo is a private residence north of Lauderdale, Mississippi.

North Carolina

Helen's Bridge

elen's Bridge in Asheville, North Carolina, is one of those manmade structures that seem imbued with the beauty and grace of nature itself. The bridge was built in 1909 to provide access to Zealandia Mansion on Beaucatcher Mountain. Its designer was R. S. Smith, who was the field architect for the Bittmore House. Smith also designed the Cathedral of All Souls in Bittmore Village. For almost a century, visitors to the site have been enchanted by the bridge. One such visitor was writer Thomas Wolfe, who often walked under the bridge as a boy in the early 1900s and shouted just to hear his echo. In 1929, he drew upon his childhood memories of Helen's Bridge for a scene in his first novel, *Look Homeward, Angel*. Over the years, Helen's Bridge has also inspired generations of teenagers, for whom a midnight visit to the old bridge in the hope of encountering Helen's ghost has become a sort of rite of passage.

According to the legend the teenagers around Asheville tell, Helen lived in a house not far from the bridge that bears her name. One day, Helen's house caught on fire. Helen tried desperately to save her daughter who was trapped inside, but the flames were too intense. Devastated by the loss of her only child, Helen ran out of her house and hanged herself from the bridge. Tessa Blythe, a twenty-year-old college student from Asheville, talked about her experiences on Helen's Bridge: "The last time I was out there was last year. We go there every Halloween. We have never really seen anything; it's just that the whole atmosphere is creepy. Every time that I have gone out there for the past five or six years, there has been something hanging from the bridge— a rope, or a rag. You're supposed to get on the bridge and throw your keys down and say, 'Helen, come forth! Helen, come forth! Helen, come forth!' I've heard that there is a light that comes straight toward you, and some people have had handprints made on their cars afterward. Some of my friends have said that they have been up there and have seen the light and, of course, they all ran. One of my friends lost his keys up there. When you throw your keys down on the road just below the bridge, you're supposed to see the light on the bridge."

Kristen Mackey, another college student from Asheville, has heard similar stories about the bridge: "You can still see the ruins of the house where her daughter died. When you go out there, you are supposed to drop your keys and say, 'Helen! Helen! Helen!' Then she is supposed to appear and float down to you. We did it one year, and it was really scary. They say there is always a rope hanging from the trestle, but I have never seen it."

Aside from hearsay, there is little historical proof for the legends of Helen's Bridge. However, the legend might have grown out of a medieval-looking residence in the area called Zealandia. Zealandia was built by John Evans Brown from Pennsylvania. After making a fortune raising sheep in New Zealand, Brown moved to Asheville in 1884. He named his castle and his 168-acre estate "Zealandia" after his adopted home. After Brown died in 1895, Zealandia was sold to O. D. Revel, who sold the home in 1904 to Sir Philip S. Henry, a well-known scholar, traveler, and patron of the arts. Just before Henry moved to his dream house, though, tragedy struck. His young wife, Violet Lewisohn, died in the Windsor Hotel fire in New York City while trying to retrieve a string of pearls from her room. It is entirely possible that the story of this tragic event somehow became tangled up in the legend of Helen. Although the castle stables burned down in 1981 while a vagabond was trying to warm himself, there is no record of an earlier fire in which Helen's daughter might have died. On the other hand, evidence of a fire could have been covered up by subsequent renovations over the years. During his twenty-nine-year stay there, Henry remodeled Zealandia several times to make it appear more "mansionesque." He even added a medieval fresco depicting Asheville landmarks, including Helen's Bridge.

After Sir Philip S. Henry died in London in 1933, Zealandia was passed down to a series of different owners. Henry's daughter Violet and her husband, General Harley H. Maconochie, lived in the castle for twenty-eight years. While the Maconochies lived there, they entertained George Gershwin, who composed part of *Rhapsody in Blue* at Zealandia. The estate was sold to George and Dottie Dixon, who were also art collectors. Mrs. Dixon told Wayne Kinser, who leases Zealandia for business purposes, that she and her husband both saw a ghost wearing black chiffon glide down the main staircase, cross the foyer, and disappear up the back staircase. After recovering from the shock of seeing a ghost, Mrs. Dixon called Violet Maconochie, who told her that the ghost was Helen's spirit. Violet advised Mrs. Dixon just to tell Helen where the Maconochies had moved and Helen would go away. Mrs. Dixon did as she was told, and Helen never appeared again.

According to another version of the legend of Helen's Bridge, Helen was the mistress of one of the castle's owners. When Helen informed her lover that she was pregnant, he flew into a fit of rage. He refused to assume responsibility for the unborn child and threw her out of the castle. Despondent, Helen walked over to the bridge and hanged herself from the rafters. There is no more historical proof for this version of the story than there is for the fire variant.

In recent years, both time and progress have imperiled the old bridge. In 1976, the North Carolina Department of Transportation decided to blast a cut through Beaucatcher Mountain to make way for Interstate 240. Even though Helen's Bridge did not stand in the path of the interstate, engineers were concerned that the concussion of the blasting might weaken the supports. To prevent the bridge from collapsing during construction of the interstate, engineers shored up the structure with support scaffolding, which remained in place for twenty-two years. In 1999, load tests were performed on the bridge to determine whether or not the scaffolding could be removed. The bridge passed the load tests, and the bridge was reopened, without the scaffolding, for pedestrian traffic only. The picturesque old bridge has rested upon the roadway so long that it has become part of the landscape, and one can only hope that it is imbued with the same kind of enduring vitality as the legend it has spawned.

Helen's Bridge is in Asheville, North Carolina. Take Vance Gap Road off Highway 26 and up Beaucatcher Mountain. Travel up the mountain until you come to a sharp bend and find a road enclosed by a narrow canyon. Helen's Bridge sits at the top of a ravine.

The North Carolina State Capitol Building

RALEIGH

*I*nterestingly enough, North Carolina did not have a fixed capital during much of the Colonial period. Legislators met in private homes and courthouses; governors lived in their own residences. The town of New Bern was selected as the seat of government in 1766, but during the Revolutionary War, the legislature deemed it safer to move from place to place. Then in 1788, a state convention voted to situate the capital on one thousand acres of Joel Lane's plantation. After a plan for Raleigh was drawn, construction of the state house began in 1792. The building served as the capitol until it burned in 1831. In 1840, the present state capitol was constructed on the site of the former state house. The cross-shaped building with a domed rotunda was originally designed by William Nichols. He was replaced by the New York architectural firm of Ithiel Town and Alexander Jackson Davis. An Edinburgh-born architect named David Paton submitted the final design in 1835, and the capitol was built under his supervision. The capitol was completed at a total cost of $532,682.34. All of North Carolina's state government agencies were housed there until 1888, when the supreme court and the state library moved to a new building. In 1963, the General Assembly moved to the state legislative building. Today, the first floor of the capitol is occupied by the governor, the lieutenant governor, and their staff. Because the state capitol did not suffer any serious damage during the Civil War, it is one of the most intact state capitols in the entire South. Some very interesting legends about the capitol have been preserved as well.

Most of the capitol legends focus around the building's unique architectural features. One legend has it that during the Civil War an escape tunnel was made for the governor's use. Although a small tunnel was built in the 1880s to connect the capitol to a heating plant across Edenton Street, no escape tunnels were ever dug under the capitol. It was also rumored that "secret rooms" within the capitol were used either by Confederate spies during the Civil War or by political spies during Reconstruction. Actually, there is some truth to these stories. When the capitol was built, there were unfinished spaces at each end of the house gallery. These spaces were inaccessible until cast-iron stairs were installed, and the upper areas were converted into additional legislative office space. However, there is no evidence that these rooms were ever used for secret purposes at any time in North

Carolina's history. Finally, there is the story that the west first- to second-floor staircase was damaged in the 1870s when whiskey barrels were rolled from floor to floor. The fact that the edges of the steps were broken from underneath lends credence to the theory that the damage occurred when wheelbarrows containing large amounts of firewood were hauled up the back staircase during legislative sessions. To date, no conclusive evidence has been uncovered to support this explanation.

Without a doubt, the most enduring of the capitol legends is the capitol ghost. Longtime night watchman Owen Jackson never saw the ghost, but he heard it many times. On many occasions, he heard books fall off the shelves, only to discover that no books were on the floor. Several times, Jackson heard doors slam behind him as he walked through the hallway. When he checked the doors, however, he found that all of them were locked. One night, the sound of breaking glass drew Jackson to the second floor, where he found all the windows perfectly intact. Jackson's most terrifying experience in the capitol took place one night while he was sitting at the visitors' entrance in the east corridor of the main floor. Suddenly, the silence was shattered by the blood-curdling scream of a woman. Jackson remained seated. "If she'd needed me," he said, "she would have screamed again."

Kevin Beck, a historical specialist at the capitol, used to kid Jackson about hearing spooky sounds in the building until he had his own encounter in the early spring of

1981 when he decided to work late: "Early on in my career, I was doing some restoration work in the state library up on the third floor of the capitol, and at least on two or three occasions, I had the feeling that you get when someone comes up a foot behind you and looks over your shoulder. It was not threatening, but it was just the feeling that someone was there who shouldn't have been there. I told the night watchman that night, 'If you see something coming down the stairs late at night, be sure you hit the second one because the first one's going to be me!'" Beck and Jackson are not the only capitol employees who have felt something strange in the old building. "There are some very strange activities here after hours," Beck said. "Most people who work here have had the sort of sixth-sense feeling that there is someone else in the room with them at night, even when they know they are alone."

Beck had another ghostly experience in November 2002 during a scientific investigation conducted at the capitol by the Rhine Research Institute. The group was taking readings in the old house chambers on the second floor, which is an area that Beck and his coworkers did not suspect as being haunted. Something very strange happened while he was being interviewed by Patty Wilson, a member of the group: "At one point during an interview I was doing with Patty, she actually saw someone sitting in the chamber behind me. I slowly turned around to see what she was seeing and could not. She described it as a nineteenth-century legislator. She said that she had only four apparitions known to her that she had seen, and this one was the most opaque of the four." After the investigation of the house chambers was completed, Beck saw the playback on the digital cameras and clearly observed orbs of energy moving up and across the chamber. "There was no trickery involved," Beck said. "There was no way light or insects could have affected what they were showing with their infrared cameras." According to Beck, the Rhine Research Institute's findings underscored two important points:

1. That everyone who has had an experience at the capitol is sane.
2. That there really is some sort of paranormal activity going on here that none of us can explain.

Kevin Beck's view toward the strange phenomena in the state capitol changed considerably after the investigation: "I have always felt like there was something going on here, but as far as being a big believer, I was not. But after the investigation, I went home with a case of the willies that I did not shake until four or five o'clock in the morning. In my twenty-six years here, it was the most bizarre evening I have ever spent in the building."

The North Carolina State Capitol Building is located at One East Edenton Street in Raleigh; phone: 919-715-4030.

Mordecai Plantation

RALEIGH

*T*he original part of the Mordecai House was built in 1785 by Joel Lane for his son and daughter-in-law, Henry and Polly Hinton Lane. After Moses Mordecai married the Lanes's daughter, Margaret, the mansion was renamed "Mordecai House." The 1826 Greek Revival addition was designed by state architect William Nichols. Five generations of the same family have resided here. In the years preceding the Civil War, the Mordecai House was situated on what was one of the largest plantations in Wake County, North Carolina. At one time, Mordecai plantation was so large that several Raleigh neighborhoods now stand on former Mordecai land. Thousands of acres of fertile farmland produced corn, cotton, wheat, and other crops. Like most plantations, Mordecai was worked almost entirely by slaves. Legend has it that one of the previous owners of the plantation, Mary Willis Mordecai Turk, is still keeping watch over her beloved home.

Tour coordinator Diana Mauney traces the source of Mordecai Plantation's haunted reputation to two sightings that occurred almost thirty years apart: "Back in the mid-1970s, we had a housekeeper here. Her name was Rosa. One morning, she was cleaning in the hallway entrance to the house. She happened to look up and see a lady walk down the hallway and go into the parlor. She was wearing a long black floor-length skirt—it was pleated—and a white, puffy shirt. She had her hair piled on top of her head. Rosa thought it was one of the volunteers. So she went into the parlor to speak to her, but she realized it must have been a ghost when there was nobody there."

The next sighting occurred in the summer of 2001 when the Mordecai House was undergoing an extensive restoration: "One early morning, a gentleman was working in the ceiling in the entry hall. He was standing upon a scaffold, and he was alone in the house—the other staff members hadn't arrived yet—and he saw the same thing Rosa did. A woman came down the stairs and opened up the French doors to the entrance hall. She went into the parlor wearing the same type of clothing Rosa described. His description matched Rosa's to a T. No one else has seen her since."

Although the ghost has never appeared again in the house, the ghostly activity continues in different ways. "There are occasions when you'll hear doors opening and closing," Mauney said. "You're not sure if you're hearing things because the house is large, and when you're downstairs and you hear something, you're not sure if you've really heard it." In the fall of 2002, a visitor from

New Zealand asked Diana about the spirit in Mary Willis Mordecai Turk's room. At the time, no one had told her about the ghost. Children seem to be particularly sensitive to the presence within the house. "Some children have been nervous when going to Mary Willis's room, which leads us to believe that this might be the ghost of Mary Willis." Mary Willis Mordecai Turk was born in the Mordecai House and married in the parlor. Her bedroom still contains many of her original furnishings.

An investigation of the Mordecai House conducted by the Rhine Institute in the fall of 2002 experienced some dramatic spikes on their EMF detectors in certain rooms within the house, an indication that some paranormal activity might be going on. Mauney says that most of the groups that have investigated the house have felt a happy presence there. "There's an overall feeling of joy," Mauney said. "They [the spirits] are happy about what we're doing about the place. There are times when you walk in the bedroom that there's a sense of warmth. I have felt that. It's almost as if we're a part of the Mordecai family. The place makes you feel warm and happy. All the letters we have mention the warmth in the home. We walk into the house in the morning and say, 'Good morning, ladies,' because so many ladies live here, and we feel like we are part of their family."

The Mordecai Historic Park is located at One Mimosa Street, Raleigh, North Carolina; phone: 919-834-4844.

Bellamy Mansion

*T*he Bellamy Mansion is one of the most magnificent antebellum homes in Wilmington, North Carolina. The stately home was built in 1859 by Dr. John D. Bellamy. Dr. Bellamy and his family had not lived in their new home for very long before the specter of a possible invasion by Union forces loomed over the city. In 1865, Federal troops took possession of Bellamy Mansion. For the remainder of the Civil War, the house was used as the headquarters for General Hawley. By the time the Bellamy family was able to reclaim their home, its elegance was destroyed. Most of the expensive furnishings were gone, and abuse and neglect were apparent everywhere. With a great deal of effort, the Bellamys restored their home and continued living there well into the twentieth century. The old house passed through a series of owners until 1972 when Bellamy Mansion Incorporated was formed to preserve it. Restoration efforts received a considerable boost in 1989 when Bellamy Mansion Incorporated combined their funds with those of the Historic Preservation Foundation of

North Carolina. Although most of the staff members at Bellamy disavow the presence of ghosts at Bellamy Mansion and do not mention them on their tours, the tales persist, thanks in large part to articles published in newspapers and books and to stories told by the night managers.

Some people believe that some of the ghost stories that have sprung up over the years have a very mundane source. For example, not long after the Bellamys moved back in their house, some of the servants reported seeing spirits in the house, including a skeleton in the basement area. The skeletal sighting can be explained by the fact that one of the Bellamy boys, Willie, brought a skeleton home with him from the medical school he attended in New York. When the mood struck him, he placed the skeleton on the ironing board in his basement office to scare the servants. It is also possible that some of the ghostly voices heard by the servants actually came from Willie's mischievous siblings.

Not all the strange occurrences at Bellamy Mansion can be explained away quite as easily, however. In later years, people driving by the old house told of seeing an elderly couple sitting in one of the upstairs windows. At the time, no one fitting their descriptions lived in the house. Others have seen a lone woman dressed in black sitting in the window. Some have speculated that this could be the ghost of Ellen, the last surviving Bellamy daughter, who died on January 30, 1946, at the age of ninety-four. In the late 1990s, a group of

Civil War reenactors said that they actually heard soldiers stomping up the stairs in their heavy boots in the middle of the night.

People who work inside the Bellamy Mansion have also had some ghostly experiences. Tim Stoltz, one of the night managers, has worked late in the evening while preparing for weddings and other special events. He claims to have seen the ghost of a man in black on the second floor: "I do a lot of weddings and these types of events. There is one ghost that's been seen on the second floor. He's called the Man in Black. We consider him to be a Union officer. The mansion was used as a field hospital during the Occupation, and he's been seen on tours walking away from people. When I first saw him, we were closing up, and I said, 'There's somebody upstairs.' The man I was with said, 'There's nobody upstairs.' We shut the house down, turned on the alarm system, went outside and waited, and nothing happened. I have seen the Man in Black a half dozen times since then."

Stoltz has never really been frightened in the house, but he has experienced some very strange phenomena at night. Once in 2002, he heard the piano play at night. That same year, he turned off the lights and set the alarms, only to find that the lights were back on as he was walking through the parking lot. Stoltz has even gotten "up close and personal" with one of the spirits in the house. On several occasions, he has slept over in the house after a wedding and had a rude awakening: "If I've had one too many, or if I'm just too tired, I'll just sleep on the couch. It'll be just about two or three in the morning, and I'll wake up, and I'll be on the floor. And I'll think, 'Well, nothing really happened.' But when I lay back down, it feels like someone grabs your pants leg and pulls down. When I was rolled off the couch, I'd say, 'Miss Ellen, leave me alone. I've had a long day. I need some sleep.' And the house quiets down. It's happened to me three or four times."

According to Stoltz, some visitors have sensed the presence of children in Bellamy Mansion: "People have heard children's laughter on the third floor. I've also had people who won't go into the corner bedroom in the children's quarters. Personally, I've never seen or felt any real presence there, just a cold chill." The lingering ghosts on the third floor could indeed be the spirits of some younger members of the Bellamy family. Not only did the Bellamys have nine children, but a number of cousins, grandchildren, nieces, and nephews also spent time in the mansion.

Some of the late-night disturbances at Bellamy Mansion have been so dramatic that even the police have gotten involved. Another night manager, Paul Bowerman, says that the local police have made several visits to the old house. One of these visits took place at ten P.M. when Bowerman received a phone call at his home informing him that the alarm system at Bellamy Mansion had been triggered and the police had been dispatched to the house: "I got down there, and several windows and doors were open. A couple of doors were open that we don't normally lock, so the police turned the dogs loose. They found nobody there. Two of the police officers helped me lock the house up, locking every window and every door. Upstairs are two windows and a door. The police officer shut and locked the windows and locked the door. The house was secure, and we all had a good laugh, and left." Convinced that the night's strange little episode had ended, Bowerman returned home. Then at three o'clock in the morning, he received another phone call telling him that the alarm was going off again: "I got down there, and it was the same police officers that were down there before, at least most of them. We got up to the second floor, and the window the policeman had shut and locked and the door next to it were open. That totally shocked him because he had locked it; I hadn't. We once again found nobody in the house." Bowerman says that sometimes, the officers on call have let the canine units walk through the house instead of doing it themselves. On another occasion, the two policemen accompanying Bowerman through the house had their guns drawn the entire time. "They were very uncomfortable, to say the least," Bowerman said.

Bowerman has also had some very strange encounters with objects in the Bellamy Mansion. One such object can be found in the master bedroom suite on the second floor. In her later years, the last surviving daughter, Ellen, was confined to a wheelchair. Because she spent all of her time here, she added a small kitchen and a bathroom. After the house was converted to a museum, workers found the wheelchair in a storage room. By examining old family photographs, workers determined that this was indeed Miss Ellen's wheelchair. The wheelchair was then placed on display in a back room on the second floor. Bowerman said that the wheelchair stayed in the back room for two weeks before it suddenly appeared in the front room, where it remained for a few days. Then, while Bowerman was giving a tour, he noticed that the wheelchair had been inexplicably returned to the back room. It did not remain there long: "One Sunday night, I was giving tours, and the wheelchair was in the back room. People were going through the house and having a good time. As I was closing the house up, I noticed that the chair was in the front room. I thought it was odd that guests would play with artifacts in the house, so I dragged it to the back room where it belonged. I put a sign on it, stating, 'Do not touch! Do not move!' The house was closed on Monday. When I got in on Tuesday morning, the chair was in the front room. I had had it! I moved the chair across the hall to the opposite front room, and it has been there for about five years now."

Another object in the house that has provided some strange thrills is a huge mirror in the back part of the house. Bowerman recalled something very strange that happened while he and another staff worker were trying to install the mirror over the mantle: "The mirror is seven feet tall and six feet wide, and it is very heavy. Putting the mirror in place is a monstrous job. I don't know how they got it off the wall in the first place in order to restore it. We were standing on scaffolding the entire time we were replacing the mirror. I was holding the mirror up, and he was on the other side, trying to anchor bolt it to the wall. All at once, he told me, 'Stop it!' I didn't know what he was talking about, so I said, 'Do you want me to let go or what?' He said, 'No, just hang onto the mirror and quit playing with me.' I said, 'Fine!' As I was holding the mirror, it felt like somebody was blowing on the back on my neck. I turned around, and there was nobody there. Then I looked over to the other guy, and he was brushing his head. He said, 'Damn it! Knock it off!' Then he looked over at me and saw that I was holding onto the other side. He finished anchoring the mirror, and as we got down from the scaffolding, he said, 'I think I've had enough today. Let's go home.'" As the two men walked out of the room, they heard the distinct sound of a child laughing. Bowerman and his partner left the room in a hurry.

Ever since the Bellamy Mansion first opened as a museum seven years ago, the staff has tried to exploit the house's haunted reputation as a means of raising money. Every Halloween, volunteers convert the old house into a "spook house" and give special tours. One year, according to Bowerman, the "ghosts" were a little too real: "Several years ago, the Actors Guild put on a haunted house on the first floor to raise some money. Most of the activity took place in one of the bedrooms. There are windows in the hallway and a door in each bedroom. Chairs were placed inside the room between the window and the door, and some of the actors were positioned at the window and at the bedroom door. As the people walked by the window going to the front of the house, little kids would reach out and grab them. On the first night, within an hour, the two kids in that room were complaining that the other one was pulling on his costume. The staircase was between them, so they could not have pulled the costume and gotten back that quickly. This went on for six weeks." By the time Halloween had arrived, the director had gone through the entire cast, and no one wanted to stay in that particular room because someone—or something—kept pulling on their costumes.

By far, the most bizarre event Bowerman witnessed occurred at one A.M. while he was closing up the house after a late party. After making sure that every door and window was locked, Bowerman walked down the second-floor hallway where he saw an apparition: "Out of the corner of my eye, I saw a man dressed in black pants and black dress shoes walk into the bedroom on the right-hand side of the house. I thought he was one of the guests left over from the reception, so I decided to go into the room and tell him, 'I'm locking up. It's time to go home.' When I entered the room, there was nobody there, so I began walking around the second floor of the house, yelling that I needed to lock up the house." After conducting a sweep of the second floor and finding nobody, Bowerman walked down to the basement and looked around. Finding no one, he did a second walk-through, this time opening all of the closets.

Finally, Bowerman looked at his watch and discovered that it was three o'clock in the morning. Tired and frustrated, he decided to end his search and go home. As he walked down the main staircase, he came face-to-face with the mysterious stranger once again: "I saw this person come out of the room on the right-hand side of the house and move down the hallway, like he was going to the room across the hall. I turned around and ran back through the back bedroom and through the closet. You can get from one room to the next by passing through the closets. There was nobody there, so I went down to the front door and set the motion detector alarm. I sat on the porch for an hour. I was so mad that I decided I was going to press charges when the police got there, but the alarms never went off, so I drove home."

The next morning, Bowerman told the story of the weird man in the house to a high school student who was learning how to do tours and supervise evening functions. The two had a good laugh and did not think about the incident again until three weeks later when the young man told Bowerman that in class that day he and his classmates were asked by their teacher to stand up, introduce themselves, and discuss one of their hobbies. After the young volunteer stood up and said that he worked at the Bellamy Mansion, a girl sitting next to him said that she would never go into that house. When asked why, she responded, "My mom broke into that house when she was in high school and saw a man in a black suit on the second floor in the hall." Bowerman was shocked but at the same time relieved that somebody had finally corroborated his story.

Additional confirmation of Bowerman's sighting of the Man in Black came a week later when he and the high school volunteer were closing up the house: "We both came off the third floor. As we turned around to walk down the hallway, we both saw a man in a black suit. He had long black hair, which was turning gray. He had a full beard. He was about as tall as I am, maybe a little shorter. He didn't look transparent or misty. He walked into the back bedroom, and the high school kid said, 'I'm sorry, Buddy, but we're closing now.' As he walked down the hall toward the man, I turned around and went into the bedroom to cut him off in the hallway. The other guy and I met each other in the back room. He was white as a sheet. He flew down the stairway and tried to get out the front door, but he was so shaken that he couldn't open it." Bowerman tried to calm down his friend by telling him that they would leave as soon as they set all of the alarms. One of the motion detectors indicated movement in the basement. The younger man declined to leave the doorway, so Bowerman checked out the basement by himself and found nothing. When Bowerman returned to the main entrance, he found his friend still "hugging" the front door. The high school student bypassed the alarm, locked the door, and left. He never worked another night with Bowerman.

Oddly enough, Tim Stoltz and Paul Bowerman are the only staff members who have had any weird experiences in the Bellamy Mansion lately, probably because they are the only ones who work at night. Although both men have had unsettling experiences in the house, neither of them is afraid to work there. Stoltz keeps his sanity by putting everything in the proper perspective: "After spending two years in Viet Nam and working in a nuclear power plant, you can't scare me with this stuff." Bowerman tends to ward off fear by resorting to humor. When people ask him why the ghosts don't scare him, he usually replies, "If a ghost ever kills me, I'll be in the same place he is. Then I'll kick his butt."

Bellamy Mansion is located at the corner of Fifth Avenue and Market Street in Wilmington, North Carolina; phone: 910-251-3700.

Chowan College

*C*howan College in Murfreesboro, a four-year coeducational institution, is the second oldest of North Carolina's seven Baptist colleges. It opened in 1848 as Chowan Baptist Female Institute, a four-year college for women. It was renamed Chowan College in 1910 and began accepting male students in 1931. Chowan College became a two-year institution in 1937 but returned to four-year status in 1992. Among the most revered of the college's traditions is the legend of the Brown Lady.

The legend of the Brown Lady exists in two forms. One of the oldest versions was recorded in the 1914 *Chowanoka*, the school annual. The story begins in September 1885. One of the many freshman girls was nineteen-year-old Eolene Davidson, the beautiful daughter of a wealthy farmer in Northampton County. A tall, slender girl with wavy black hair, fair complexion, and blue eyes, Eolene was popular at school and beloved at home. She roomed in what is now the Administration

Building. The previous summer, Eolene was visiting her friend Margaret Lanston at New York when she met a handsome twenty-five-year-old lawyer named James Lorrene. After several months, James asked Eolene to become his bride. Eolene wanted to say "yes," but she had to decline his offer because her father wanted her to earn a college education. With tears in her eyes, Eolene told her lover that she would marry him after she graduated from college.

Eolene kept her love affair a secret from her parents until the night she was to leave for school. Fighting back the tears, she told her mother about James's proposal and her decision to put off marriage until she graduated. After Eolene had finished, her mother threw her arms around her daughter's neck and praised her for acting so sensibly. Eolene enjoyed her first year at Chowan College. Although studying came first, Eolene always found time to socialize with her friends at school. By the time her first year ended, she had earned the nickname "the Lady in Brown" because of her preference for dresses made of brown silk. During the summer, James visited Eolene, and the couple's love became stronger than ever.

The next summer, Eolene returned to Chowan, more determined than ever to pursue her studies. Eolene excelled in all of her courses until the middle of October, when she was stricken with fever. Despite the best efforts of the medical staff at the college, Eolene's condition worsened until she finally passed away on Halloween.

The next day, her body was returned to her parents. Every fall from that time until the present, many freshmen at Chowan have heard the faint rustling of the silk skirts of the Brown Lady as she roams the dark halls of the Administration Building.

Another version of the tale was expressed in the form of a poem written in 1928 by Ethleen G. Vick, Class of 1928. In Ms. Vick's poem, the Brown Lady was a young woman who fell in love with a young man who disapproved of the southern cause and rode off to fight with the Union army. His love for her was so strong, he told her before they parted that "tho death should o'er take me, I'll come back some way/To claim you my darling if God says I may" (McKnight and Creech 1964, 169). The young woman waited patiently for her lover to return until one day, she received a message informing her that her lover had died in battle. After reading the letter, she was so grief-stricken that she had a heart attack and died at twelve midnight. The poem ends with a salute to the enduring power of true love:

> So if you hear rustlings on the stairs, thru the hall
> Or see her go tripping thru the pines in the fall
> Or, if by chance, you should see her one night
> Stroll 'neath the pines in the melting moonlight
> She'll be keeping her "tryst" with her lover, they say,
> For she knows he'll come back as he promised that day.
> (169)

Another graduate of Chowan College, Martha Yates Seymour (Class of 1937), wrote an essay about the Brown Lady's first appearance. Around the turn of the century, Dr. McDowell told the students that they could worship at home because of the cold, snowy weather and then went up to his office, which is now part of the infirmary. Dr. McDowell's office was right across the hall from the apartment where he and his wife lived. After standing in the door of his office for a few minutes, he entered his apartment and asked his wife, "Mary, who is that lady who came in the office a few minutes ago?" His wife replied that no one had entered his office. Dr. McDowell then insisted that a young lady had passed by him in the hallway, quickly entered the office, and left just as fast. He added that she had a worried expression and wore a brown dress. Later that afternoon, Dr. Delk, the science teacher, came up to Dr. McDowell's office and asked, "Who was the young lady that was just up here?" The professor went on to say that she had beckoned to him as she came out of the parlor door. Dr. Delk walked down the hall to speak to her, but by the time he reached the parlor, she was gone. He then went outside to look for her footprints in the snow but found nothing. Dr. McDowell replied that there was no one up there. A year or two later on a hot July afternoon, Dr. McDowell left his desk and walked into the adjoining room. There, he was confronted once again with a vision of the Brown Lady. She beckoned him to follow her, but when he went out into the hall, he saw no one. Then his gaze was drawn to a windowsill on the west window where a squirrel cage was twirling rapidly. When Dr. McDowell walked over to investigate, he was shocked to discover that the squirrel was dead.

Some intriguing college traditions have grown up around the Brown Lady in the past one hundred years. In the conclusion of her essay, Ms. Seymour stated that during the Brown Lady's appearance at the college each year, she tests the loyalty of the students and instills the spirit of loyalty in each freshman. In the 1940s and 1950s, Chowan College celebrated their campus ghost in a Brown Lady Festival, during which a student was nominated to dress up as the Brown Lady. At first, legend had it that she returned each October, but later, the time was fixed as Halloween. Festival goers usually wound up at the old Wise Family Cemetery, located across the ravine from the college. The purpose of the festival was to imbue each new student class with pride and ideals. One of Chowan's presidents, W. B. Edwards, went so far as to have the students driven westward across College Creek to the Wise Family Cemetery. For years, freshman girls told stories of hearing the rustling of the lady's brown silk taffeta dress during her annual visit to the college. Some students said that she died of typhoid fever. Others swore that she died of a broken heart. The Brown Lady might be gone, but her name still comes up in freshmen orientation and when leaves and twigs are found in the halls of the Administration Building the next morning after it has been locked up for the night.

Chowan College is in Murfreesboro, North Carolina; phone: 252-398-6500.

South Carolina

Hampton Plantation

*t*he Hampton Plantation in Georgetown, South Carolina, was built by a family of French Huguenots in 1735. The original house was a one-and-a-half story, central hall structure. In 1757, the house was enlarged to its present size by Daniel Horry. After Horry died in 1785, his second wife, Harriott Pickney Horry, inherited the house. The pediment and wide portico were added to the front of the house in 1790. The Hampton Plantation's most illustrious visitor was George Washington, who ate breakfast there in 1791. The last owner of the Hampton Plantation, author and state poet laureate Archibald Rutledge, left the family home and property to the state. Now the locus of Hampton Plantation State Park, the old house still resonates with the tragic end of one of Archibald Rutledge's ancestors.

Tour guide Sarah Tyler says that the haunting of Hampton Plantation has traditionally been linked with John Henry Rutledge: "John Henry Rutledge was twenty-one years old in 1830, and he had fallen in love with a girl in Georgetown. Her father was a pharmacist. John Henry's family were planters, and the two different classes don't mix. Both families were against them getting married or involved. The girl ended up marrying someone else, and John Henry decided that life wasn't worth living, so he shot himself. He didn't shoot himself very well, so he didn't die right away. He lingered for a few days before dying. He's not buried in the cemetery because it's considered a sin to commit suicide, so he's actually buried on the grounds right outside the front door. We think where his grave marker is now was moved by the last owner."

Not surprisingly, much of the ghostly activity in the old house emanates from John Henry's bedroom. "People have said that in his room, which is upstairs, they have heard the sound of a rocking chair and sounds of him crying," Tyler explains. This is the very chair that John Henry Rutledge was sitting in when he shot himself with a sawed-off shotgun in March 1830. Rumors about the rocking chair sprung up several years later when a servant heard a chair rocking in the upstairs library. She ran up the stairs to investigate and found the chair rocking by itself. Supposedly, there is also a blood-stain on the floor by the rocking chair that has resisted all attempts to be scrubbed off.

Over the years, other strange things have happened at Hampton Plantation, according to Sarah Tyler: "The manager here has said that he'll lock doors and come back and the doors are unlocked. He said he has turned off all the lights in the house, and as he was driving away, he looked back at the house, and the lights were back on." Some visitors standing in the dining room area claim to have heard three distinct raps and the sound of a body being dragged from a northwest to a southeast corner of the upstairs bedroom."

John Henry Rutledge was not the only person to die in the house. "The first owner, Daniel Horry, actually died here in the house of liver disease," Tyler said, "and it wasn't a pretty ending. He was in lot of pain. His tongue was encrusted, his skin was yellow, he had a fever, and he had the hiccups. So he could be the ghost. He did not die of old age. He had a disease. If you're going to explore all the options, you've got to consider that Daniel might be the ghost. I'm not aware of anyone else dying here."

Sarah Tyler believes that the ghost legends surfaced when the park first opened. In the early days, the old house was not staffed as it is today: "People were just allowed to go through the house. There might have been somebody here to take your money. We were so tucked away that not very many people knew about us, so we only had a couple of people coming in per day. These were the people who described the rocking chair rocking or the crying. They would tell the manager that they heard these things, and when he'd ask them which room the sounds came from, they always described the same room. The manager was freaked out because they all heard the same thing in the same room."

Even though Sarah Tyler has worked at Hampton Plantation State Park for two years, she has never felt or heard anything out of the ordinary. In fact, she has never felt scared in the house, even though she has stayed there alone many times. Still, she is not prepared to dismiss all the stories she has heard as nonsense: "The other interpreter refuses to stay here after dark. I don't doubt that something is happening, but I've never seen it."

Hampton Plantation is nineteen miles south of Georgetown on U.S. Route 17. The address is Hampton Plantation, 1950 Rutledge Road, McClellanville, SC 29458; phone: 843-546-9361.

Poogan's Porch

CHARLESTON

oogan's Porch is one of Charleston's finest restaurants. The house that was converted into Poogan's Porch was built in 1886. For many years, it was the home of a lonely woman named Zoe St. Amand. Zoe spent most of her adult life in the bottom half of this house with her sister, Liz St. Amand. Zoe never married, choosing instead to nurture the children she taught at the Craft's House School, which stood just up the street on the corner of Queen and Legare Streets. Zoe outlived Liz by nine years and died alone in the house. In 1976, Bobbie Ball purchased the old apartment building with the intention of turning it into a restaurant. As she was moving in, Bobbie discovered that the previous owners had left behind their dog, Poogan. The Yorkshire terrier stayed on, greeting customers from his place on the front porch until his death in 1979. In the next few years, Bobbie learned that something else came with the house at 72 Queen Street besides a cute little dog.

Bobbie Ball and her coworkers soon found out that something was not "quite right" about the restaurant as far back as the 1970s. Some customers and workers said they felt someone brush up against them in a room where no one else was present. Others reported seeing a very old woman who took a seat at one of the less conspicuous booths. They said that she vanished almost as soon as anyone took notice of her. One of these witnesses was a pregnant woman who was in the bathroom when she saw an elderly lady in black disappear before her very eyes. Guests staying on the second floor at the Mills House Hotel have seen an old lady standing in a second-floor window long after the restaurant has closed for the evening. Some especially distraught witnesses have even called the police department to report seeing an old woman trapped in Poogan's Porch after hours. Over the years, a few employees have quit because the shock of meeting Zoe was more than they could bear.

One employee who had a ghostly experience in the restaurant was Bobbie Ball's stepfather, who comes in from time to time to do maintenance work. He usually arrives at four A.M. before the other employees begin reporting for work at six. On one particular morning, her stepfather began making a fresh pot of coffee when he noticed there were no styrofoam cups. He went upstairs, got a fresh stack of styrofoam cups, and poured himself a cup of coffee. After setting his coffee cup at the end of the bar, he walked right around the corner to do some plumbing in the men's room. At around six o'clock, he heard noises coming from the bar area. Thinking that Bobbie had come in early, he finished what he was doing and walked into the bar. He was surprised to find that half his coffee was gone, and there were lipstick prints on the cup.

Poogan's Porch has undergone several periods of construction since first opening in 1976. Ball has remodeled several times and built on an addition to the restaurant. Over the years, she has observed that the haunted activity seems to escalate whenever the construction crews arrive. One particularly violent incident took place in December 2001 when the restaurant was closed for two weeks while the kitchen was being remodeled: "It was about four in the evening, and all of the construction crew had left. I was getting ready to lock up. Another girl was in here. I couldn't get the security codes set on the alarm set, so I called ADT, which is our alarm company, and I said, 'I can't get the alarm set.' So they said, 'Go upstairs and try that door upstairs. Make sure it's locked.' So I sent the young lady upstairs while I hung on the phone with him. I'm standing in the doorway between the hostess foyer and the bar area. There was nobody else in the building. All the doors were locked. All of a sudden, a bar stool came flying across the room. It knocked over a couple of other bar stools. And then it was like someone was standing by the kitchen door, which was a good way from these bar stools, by the way. It wasn't like the bar stool hit the kitchen door. It was a good ten feet away from them. It was like someone took their foot and kicked the kitchen door open. It made a good, loud bang. That door was swinging back and forth. It made such a commotion that the ADT guy heard it on the phone, and he said, 'What in the world's going on?' And I said, 'Oh my gosh! I think I'm being robbed' because I thought someone had been kneeling down in the bar and run into the kitchen. I said, 'Don't hang up.' By that time, the other girl had walked down the stairs. She saw the whole thing as well. She said, 'Bobbie, that's the ghost.' She had had a couple of ghostly encounters before and she wasn't all that frightened. I said, 'There's no way I'm walking into that kitchen.' There was only one door, and I knew it was locked. So I knew that whoever went into that kitchen was still in there. She said, 'There's no one in that kitchen.' I was still on the phone with the ADT, and I was stretched very close to the front door, ready to run. She calmly walked into the kitchen and turned on the lights, and, of course, there was nobody there. Now this door that was swinging back and forth is a very heavy antique wooden door. It's not like one of those flimsy metal doors like you see in restaurants. Our waiters have to use their shoulders or their foot to open it. Right then, I said, 'Oh, my goodness!' That was pretty crazy." Ball believes that Zoe becomes very agitated whenever structural changes are being made to her beloved home.

A similar incident occurred when air conditioning was being installed in the kitchen. The construction crew came in at midnight because they were going to work all night. A couple of weeks later, Greg, the owner of the air-conditioning company, came in with the invoice and said, "Oh, by the way, you know, you've got a ghost." Sensing that the man had not heard the ghost stories, Ball said, "Yeah, I know. How did you find out?" He said that the previous night, Bob, one of the workers, had gone over to the bar to pour himself a Coke from the fountain. He was standing at the bar, and when he looked at the back bar stairs, he saw an old woman in a black dress standing there. After a few seconds she just kind of faded. It scared him, and he went back in the kitchen and said, "Are we the only ones who are supposed to be in the restaurant?" Greg said, "Yeah, we're locked in." Bob replied, "There's an old lady on the back stairs!" The terrified man refused to go back there and work. The other workers teased him for the rest of the night, not knowing that Poogan's Porch really was haunted.

More poltergeist activity occurred in March 2003. Ball said that three of her regular customers were sitting at their usual place at the bar and eating their lunch. Bobbie's partner, John Ball, was standing at the end of the bar, watching for customers. All of a sudden, a coffee cup—kind of a café latte cup—floated off the shelf. "It was about three shelves up from the bar," Bobbie said. "It just floated off the bar and fell to the floor. It didn't just topple off because the cooler sticks beyond the shelf, and if the cup had just fallen off the shelf, it would have hit the cooler. The cup just floated out and dropped to the middle of the floor, which was about two and a half feet. This means the cup would have had to come straight out and then drop. Our customer saw it, and she said, 'Oh my God! Did you see that?' And Chuck, my partner, said, 'Oh my God! I saw it!' They both went on and started kidding each other, and then Chuck said, 'Well, she was aiming for you.' That was kind of weird." Over the years, the staff and customers at Poogan's Porch have found humor to be the best resort when rational explanations fail.

Interestingly enough, Poogan's Porch's ghostly reputation has been publicized only since 1997. "The ghost thing didn't really get played upon until five or six years ago at the most," Ball says. "They started ghost tours at Charleston, and word got out that we had a ghost. Somehow, they ran us down from stories from different people." Having a ghost in the restaurant has been good for business. In fact, Bobbie has become somewhat attached to Zoe. "She's really a friendly ghost, most of the time," Bobbie says.

Poogan's Porch is located at 72 Queen Street in Charleston; phone: 843-577-2477.

Hobkirk Hill

CAMDEN

*t*he headless horseman first entered America's consciousness in 1820 with the publication of Washington Irving's classic short story "The Legend of Sleepy Hollow." However, the Hudson Valley is not the only region that can lay claim to being the "stomping grounds" of this horrific villain. South Carolina, for example, has two headless ghosts who have been striding through the nightmares of impressionable minds for over two hundred years. One of these is the ghost of a Prussian sentry who was beheaded by one of Francis Marion's cavalrymen outside Wedgewood Plantation in Georgetown. Another regionally known specter is the headless horseman of Hobkirk Hill in Camden, South Carolina.

Hobkirk Hill is a ridge running east and west for a half mile in the northern part of present-day Camden. In 1781, it was the site of a fierce confrontation between the Continental army and the British army. At stake was the possession of the interior of South Carolina. Lord Cornwallis had left Lord Rawdon in charge at Camden while he pursued General George Washington in Virginia. Sensing that Rawdon was vulnerable, General Nathanael Greene decided to attack the Camden fortifications. Greene changed camp several times, locating at Log Town first, then moving southeast of Camden to Paint Hill. On April 19, 1781, Greene arrived within a mile of Lord Rawden's entrenchments. After determining that Rawdon's works were impregnable, Greene withdrew to Hobkirk Hill, where he awaited reinforcements. On the night of April 24, a drummer deserted to the British forces and informed Rawdon of Greene's weakness. Rawdon, whose provisions were nearly exhausted, realized that his only chance of victory against Greene's superior numbers was a surprise attack.

At dawn on April 25, Greene's cavalry pitched camp after being on duty all night. Most of them had unsaddled their horses and stacked their arms before they drank coffee or washed their clothes. Greene and his staff took breakfast at a spring on the eastern slope of Hobkirk Hill. Meanwhile, Rawdon and his garrison marched in complete silence along the margin of a swamp and up the path of Pine Tree Creek. Rawdon's men were only a mile away from Greene's camp before being spotted by American pickets, who signaled a warning with musket fire. As the pickets fell back upon the hill, they continued firing to give their troops time to organize. By this time, Rawdon had gained the left flank of the Americans. Greene quickly assembled his men into battle-line formation. Some were only partially dressed, a few were even barefooted, but they still managed to organize themselves into the familiar Cowpens–Guilford Court House pattern, with the militia out front.

As the British troops moved slowly up the slope, with a narrow front, the regiments of Campbell and Ford turned their flanks. Colonel John Gunby's Marylanders readied themselves to attack the front. Under Greene's command, the artillery pummeled the British line. Just as an American victory seemed imminent, Captain Beatty, commander of a company of Gunby's veterans, was killed, causing his raw troops to panic. Rawdon's troops broke through the center, forcing Greene to retreat. Fortunately for the Americans, George Washington's cavalry turned upon Greene's pursuers, protecting the retreating troops from the British advance. Washington also assisted Greene in the rescue of his cannon. The entire battle lasted less than half an hour. Each side lost fewer than 270 men. Although Greene had left the field of battle to the British, Rawdon was unable to replenish his losses and was forced to withdraw to a consolidated position at Charleston.

Although many people died during the Battle of Hobkirk Hill, one particular tragedy is remembered to this day. One mounted soldier who was charging the British was struck by a cannonball, which completely separated his head from the rest of his body. The man's horse was unharmed, though, and it raced off with the headless trunk of its rider still firmly seated in the saddle. As his comrades stared in horror, the horse fled across Camden and disappeared into swamps surrounding the Black River road. To this day, people say that when the swamp is covered with a misty fog on the night of the full moon, a decapitated ghost, mounted on a skeletal horse, gallops around the swamp, rides up through the cemetery and the surrounding countryside, and returns at dawn to his watery haunts. Apparently, the miserable specter is still searching for his missing head. This tale is clearly a legend that has been passed down from generation to generation in Camden. However, the soldier's tragic end has been verified by Camden historians, who mentioned it in *Historic Camden*, the history of Camden and the surrounding area.

Today, Hobkirk Hill is barely recognizable as a battle-field. The entire area is covered by upper–middle–class homes, including the ridge along which the battle was fought. In fact, were it not for the battle markers, a visitor to the area would probably never dream that over five hundred soldiers died here. In Camden, the memory of the battle is kept alive in history books, reenactments, and the legend of the headless horseman of Hobkirk Hill.

From Charlotte, take I-77 to SC Route 34 east toward Ridgeway into Lugoff, then on to Camden. Turn right at the light onto 421. Pass through downtown and stay on this road. The historic area is on the left.

The Court Inn

CAMDEN

"When beggars die, there are no comets seen. The heavens themselves blaze forth the death of princes." Dramatic changes in the human order had been predicated by omens long before Shakespeare penned these lines in his play *Julius Caesar*. In ancient Egypt, the Pharoah's dream of seven fat cows and seven lean cows foreshadowed the seven years of rich harvest followed by seven years of famine. In 1865, President Abraham Lincoln dreamed of his own funeral shortly before his assassination. For over a century, a large black cat has been sighted in the Capitol building in Washington, D.C., just before a national tragedy, such as the assassination of President John F. Kennedy on November 22, 1963. In Camden, South Carolina, the appearance of the Gray Lady at one of the city's oldest homes was interpreted as a warning of impending doom.

The story of the Gray Lady begins in France in 1572. A beautiful young woman named Eloise DeSaurin fell in love with a handsome Huguenot. The couple had planned to be married, but their dreams of wedded bliss were shattered when Eloise's father, Darce DeSaurin, found the young lovers together. A devout Catholic who hated the Huguenots, Darce became so enraged that he drew his dagger and lunged at Eloise's lover. The girl threw herself between her father and her fiancé. She promised to renounce the young man forever if her father would spare his life. Darce consented, and the young Huguenot walked out of Eloise's life forever.

Darce DeSaurin was not content simply to break up his daughter's budding romance. To ensure that she never saw her lover again, he placed Eloise in a convent. Half-mad with grief, Eloise cried out from her cell, "May the torture you have caused me to suffer recoil on you and yours forever, for the descendants of such a tyrant ill deserve happiness and peace." After wasting away in her cell for several weeks, Eloise fell ill and died of a broken heart. A faithful nun who had tended to the dying girl sent Eloise's mother a lock of her hair and a crayon portrait of her dead daughter. The news of her daughter's death was more than the distraught mother could bear. She lingered a while, and then she too died. On her death bed, she accused her husband of murdering their daughter.

For several weeks, Darce sank into a deep depression. One day, Darce decided to end his suffering by stabbing himself in the chest. A messenger was immediately dispatched to Darce's estranged sons, both of whom had embraced the Protestant faith. Raoul and Jules DeSaurin arrived home just in time to hear their father's last words. With fading breath, he said that Eloise's spirit had appeared to him and chastised him for ruining her life. Unable to live with the truth of the role he had played in his daughter's demise, Darce committed suicide.

Following their father's death, Raoul and Jules moved into the family home. One night Eloise's ghost appeared in a nun's gray garments. The men perceived that her lips were moving as if she was trying to tell them something. Without uttering a single word, Eloise vanished. When Raoul retired for the night, he found a monk's garments on the floor of his room. The next day, his brother Jules became one of 50,000 Protestants who perished in the St. Bartholomew's Day Massacre. Raoul escaped his brother's fate by donning the monk's robe that had mysteriously appeared in his room and fleeing the city.

Raoul immigrated to the United States, where he raised a family. One of his sons, also named Raoul, settled down at Camden. Eventually, Raoul's descendants took up residence in a luxurious mansion that had been christened "Lausanne" by Major John McPherson DeSaussure after his ancestral home in Switzerland. Soon, rumors began circulating that DeSaussure had brought with him to Lausanne the family ghost. According to one family legend, another Raoul DeSaussure was living at Lausanne when he became engaged to a young woman named Nina Beaumont. On one of her overnight visits to the house, Nina found herself unable to sleep. Dressed in her wrapper and slippers, she started walking down the hall to see if her friend Lucia, another guest at the house, was up as well. Nina had no sooner left her room than she felt a cold draft of air that cut through her thin gown and caused her candle to flicker. Gazing into a shaft of moonlight, Nina made out a misty figure several paces ahead moving slowly toward the stairs. Thinking that the woman was another guest suffering from insomnia, Nina started to say "Hello" when she observed that the woman was gliding, not walking, down the hallway. She was clearly wearing a long gray veil. As chills ran up Nina's spine, the gray figure reached the top of the stairs, paused, and commenced to weeping, her face buried in her hands. Without warning, the melancholy specter vanished. Nina rushed back to her room and huddled under the covers, shaking uncontrollably until she finally drifted into a fitful sleep.

Nina's first thought when she awoke the next morning was that she had dreamed about her encounter with the Gray Lady. Then she noticed that she was still wearing her wrapper and slippers. Suddenly, she remembered that the appearance of the Gray Lady spells death for members of the DeSaussure family. When she found out that Raoul was planning to go hunting that day, she begged him to stay home, but he laughed at her foolishness and rode off with his companions. After he had left, Nina went to the garden where his mother was supervising the planting of a circle of young cedar trees. The elderly black man who was planting the trees warned Mrs. DeSaussure that "when you plants cedars, you plants trouble," meaning that someone close to her would perish. Nina added her concerns to the gardener's plea and convinced Raoul's mother not to plant the cedars. Then Raoul's father, Major DeSaussure, who had overheard the women from inside the house, mocked them for being so superstitious and ordered the gardener to continue planting the cedars. However, he changed his mind regarding the power of omens later that evening upon learning that Raoul had been accidentally shot and killed by a member of his hunting party.

After Major DeSaussure's death, Lausanne was purchased in 1884 by Mrs. Caroline Jumelle Perkins, a niece of Mrs. John C. McRae, whose husband had built the mansion in 1830. "Miss Callie," as Ms. Perkins was known, "immediately undertook the enormous task of repairing and refurbishing the neglected mansion and opened it as a tourist resort in 1889. For reasons unknown, the resort was originally called "Ufton Court." Miss Callie ran the resort until her death in 1899. In 1900, Caleb Ticknor purchased the resort, made extensive renovations, and reopened it as Court Inn. The Court Inn enjoyed its greatest prosperity between 1900 and 1940, mainly because it was the nearest southern resort for many northern patrons. When business began to dwindle off, the Ticknors sold the Court Inn in the 1940s. It had several owners until brothers David and Benjamin Cromer bought it in 1960. The Cromers did extensive renovation and redecoration, but they still could not turn a profit. In late 1963, two young Camden businessmen, Guy Hutchins Jr. and Jack Karesh, purchased the Court Inn and its surrounding 5.7 acres. Soon afterward, they announced plans to dismantle the old mansion and redevelop the property, dividing it into twelve or thirteen plots. The Kershaw County Historical Society Association attempted to raise the $35,000 purchase price but failed. The old house was razed on June 10, 1964.

The Gray Lady made several appearances in the Court Inn for years before it was demolished. Her last appearance was in 1964 just a few months before the Court Inn was razed. A guest at the inn reported having seen her moving along a dimly lighted corridor. Perhaps her appearance was a warning that the Court Inn was doomed, just as early members of the DeSaussure family had been.

Hopsewee Plantation

GEORGETOWN

*O*verlooking the beautiful Santee River, Hopsewee Plantation was operated as a rice plantation until the Civil War. The Hopsewee Plantation House in Georgetown, South Carolina, was built between 1733 and 1740 by the Lynch family. The house has four rooms opening into a wide center hall on each floor. Constructed of black cypress, the house sits on a brick foundation covered by scored tabby. The pine floors are one and one-half inches thick. Furnished with eighteenth- and nineteenth-century furniture, the Hopsewee Plantation House looks much as it did when it was first built. According to witnesses, at least one of the early owners of Hopsewee can also be found inside and outside of the house.

The most illustrious owners of Hopsewee were Thomas Lynch Sr. and his son, Thomas Lynch Jr. Thomas Lynch Sr. (1726–1776) was married to Elizabeth Allston of Brookgreen Plantation. The couple had two daughters, Sabina (b. 1747) and Esther (b. 1748), and a son, Thomas Lynch Jr. (b. 1749). Thomas Lynch Sr. was not only one of the most prominent planters on the Santee River, but he was also a distinguished public servant. He was the first president of the Winyah Indigo Society founded in 1755. He served on the 1765 Stamp Act Congress and was elected to the First Continental Congress in Philadelphia in 1774. Lynch was appointed as an advisor to General George Washington in 1775. Thomas Lynch Jr.'s involvement in politics began in 1776 when his father became paralyzed as a result of a cerebral hemorrhage and the younger Lynch was selected to serve with Thomas Lynch Sr. on the Continental Congress. At the age of twenty-six, Thomas Lynch Jr. became the fifty-second signer of the Declaration of Independence. After Thomas Lynch Sr. died in 1776 while returning to South Carolina, the younger Lynch retired from public life because of a fever he had contracted during his service with the South Carolina militia in 1775. He and his wife, Elizabeth, lived at Peachtree Plantation on the South Santee River until 1779, when the young couple left for France by way of the West Indies. Only five families have owned Hopsewee in over two hundred years. However, it is the Lynch family who seems to have exerted the strongest hold on the old plantation.

Raejean Beattie, who runs the plantation, believes that Thomas Lynch Sr. is still an active presence at

Hopsewee. In fact, Ms. Beattie's neighbor, Bill Weaver, had a personal encounter with Lynch on the road one evening: "This happened last fall [2002]. I live just below Hopsewee in Crow Hill Plantation. Coming from the east going to the west, there used to be what they called Washington's Trail. My son and I were both out in the yard one evening just before dusk when we saw Thomas Lynch Sr. come down that road. He was dressed in Colonial-period clothing and carrying a lantern. He was wearing an old-fashioned hat. His most outstanding feature was his round face. His face reminded me of a basketball. He crossed over my property and went into the swamp. We looked over there at him and looked at each other and said, 'I didn't see that. Did you?' "Weaver went on to say that at one time, Lynch owned the land that is now Crow Hill Plantation.

Ms. Beattie had her own encounter at Hopsewee several years ago shortly after moving in: "My piano had just been moved into the house. I happened to be there by myself that evening. I sat down to play. It was really the first time after having been there for a year and a half that I felt like somebody was watching me. It wasn't a bad feeling. I don't think we have a bad ghost here. It was like the ghost was saying, 'Well, it's about time we had some music around here.' "

The ghost's fondness for music reasserted itself one night in February 2003. Her husband had gotten up to go to the bathroom. The family cat was in another bedroom on the bed: "He came back to bed and said, 'The cat's in the house in the other bedroom.' At about that time, the piano played. It wasn't a tune or anything. It was just a couple of notes. It would have been amazing to me for the cat to have gotten down the stairs that quickly and actually made it to the piano and jumped up on it. That could have happened, but I just prefer to think that somebody's notes made it through."

Hopsewee's ghost revealed its modest side when a crew from the Grenada Film Company arrived one day: "The costume mistress took pictures of the girls she was dressing, and all of the pictures turned out reasonably well except for the picture she took of these ladies in their stays and chemises. In that picture, they were standing in the corner of the bedroom where the light wasn't shining in the corner. The picture was in the middle of the roll, and there was this white streak through the middle of the picture that covered up everything from just below the neck to down about the knees so that you could not see the stays and chemises, so it was a very unusual picture."

Like many people who live in historically haunted houses, Raejean Beattie does not feel threatened by her ghost: "It definitely feels like it's somebody who's glad to have us there taking care of the house the way it's supposed to be taken care of." Sometimes, as she is telling her ghost stories, Raejean wishes that something even more extraordinary had happened to her: "The experiences I've had seem less spectacular than other stories, like the ghosts at Hampton. I haven't embellished anything. That's the way it really was. If I was going to make something up, I'd make it more spectacular than that."

Tennessee

Shiloh Battlefield

*O*ne of the bloodiest battles of the entire Civil War bears the unlikely name of "Shiloh," which is the Hebrew word for "peace." On April 6–7, 1862, over 23,000 soldiers died on the field of honor. General Ulysses S. Grant later recalled a field "so covered with dead that it would have been impossible to walk across the clearing . . . stepping on dead bodies without a foot touching the ground." Shiloh was indeed the realm of the dead on those two bloody days in April 1862. According to some visitors and park employees, it still is.

Just prior to the Battle of Shiloh, Union forces had begun to reverse the humiliating defeats suffered at the outset of the Civil War, thanks in large part to the tenacity of General Grant. Following Union victories at Fort Henry on the Tennessee River and Fort Donelson on the Cumberland, Grant began moving up the Tennessee with 45,000 men. By early April, Grant and his men had arrived at Pittsburg Landing, a small riverboat settlement a few miles from a little Methodist meeting house known as Shiloh Church. While awaiting a second Union army under Major General Don Carlos Buell, many of Grant's soldiers rested in the woods. Grant and his division commanders believed it would be bad for morale to have the men entrench. On the morning of April 6, 1862, Grant himself was eating breakfast at Cherry Mansion in Savannah. No one really expected the Confederates to attack.

Confederate general Albert Sidney Johnston realized that his only hope of victory was to strike before Buell's army reached Shiloh. At six A.M., three lines of Confederates charged out of the woods. The element of surprise initially worked to the Confederates' benefit. One Union officer ran back to camp shouting, "The Rebels are out there thicker than fleas on a dog's back!" Some Union soldiers were still in their tents when the shooting started. Still, most of the Union forces did not panic. They immediately began taking up a series of defensive lines to slow the Confederate attacks. By late morning, Union troops had taken a position running from the bluffs of the Tennessee River, along an abandoned farm road through a place called the Hornets' Nest, and extending to the high ground overlooking Owl Creek. Johnston directed a series of attacks against the Union troops holding the area around a peach orchard. Johnston was killed at about 2:30, and General P. G. T. Beauregard assumed command. Eleven separate assaults were also made against the Hornets' Nest at the center of the line. Grant had ordered General Lew Wallace and General Benjamin Prentiss to hold this sector at all costs. Before long, the fire from the Confederates' sixty-two cannon proved to be too much. Two Union divisions broke for the rear. Wallace was killed, and Prentiss, along with 2,100 Union soldiers from the Second and Sixth divisions, surrendered.

Completely overwhelmed by Confederate forces, Grant established a final defensive line, stretching from Dill Branch on the left, over to the Corinth Road in the center, and ending at Tilghman Branch on the right. This line provided protection for Pittsburg Landing, where Buell's men were arriving. The Confederates attempted to attack the line by descending a sixty-foot bluff, crossing the marshy bottom of the ravine, and climbing the bank on the far side. Two Confederate brigades gained a toehold on the bank of the ravine, but they could not hold it and were forced to retreat.

When morning came, Grant had Buell's 25,000 fresh troops to throw into the battle. Besides Buell's troops, General Lew Wallace's division had arrived as well. Outnumbered and exhausted from the night-long bombardment, the Confederates were forced to fall back. By midafternoon, they had begun an orderly retreat. Because the Union troops were too weary to pursue them, the Confederates were able to reach Corinth later that evening. The battle ended with both sides suffering grievous losses. The Union lost 13,000 men, the Confederates 10,000.

Not surprisingly, a large number of paranormal events have been reported at Shiloh down through the years. One of these stories centers around a site with the ominous name of "Bloody Pond." During the battle, hundreds of soldiers crawled and dragged themselves to the pond for a drink of water; many of them drowned there because they were too battle weary to raise their heads out of the water. By the end of the second day of battle, the pond had turned red from the blood of the horses and soldiers who died there. It is said that sometimes the pond still turns red, although the red tinge in the water might be caused by the rays of the sun. Another story has it that the ghosts are active at the old caretaker's home, where people have reported hearing ghostly voices and footsteps and seeing doors open and close by themselves. Others have claimed to hear distant gunfire and the sounds of marching feet, a phenomenon that has been reported at other battlefields as well.

One of the stories that the rangers at Shiloh tell centers around a Confederate burial trench located on the battlefield. The trench is located between Water Oaks Pond and Crescent Field. Many of these soldiers buried here were killed on April 5, 1862. Jeffrey Gentsch, an expert on the Battle of Shiloh, tells the story as it was given to him: "The story has it that at certain times of day—generally before dusk—people have noticed a soldier of the Civil War era walking in the ravine in a tattered uniform. The ravine separates Water Oaks Pond and Crescent Field. People say that he usually appears for two or three minutes, which is a fairly long sighting."

Another Confederate soldier made a totally unexpected appearance several years ago when Bonnie Hallman and Sandy Watson were walking through Shiloh on a lovely peaceful day: "A group of us went up to Shiloh because we love history and old battlefields. There is long row of cannons overlooking the field. The field is surrounded by a perimeter of forest. We were walking along the edge of the woods, and Sandy giggled and reached over and elbowed me. She said, 'Look over there.' I did, and there was a kid asleep wearing a Confederate uniform. He was lying down on the moss with his knees up. He had one arm lying on his cheek and one arm at his side with his hat over his face. I said, 'Is he sleeping it off from last night? Is he O.K.? He appears to be O.K.' We stood there watching the kid. It was sort of a strange thing to find in the woods. And then he wasn't there. He just dissolved in the air."

Shiloh's most famous ghost is undoubtedly the Drummer Boy of Shiloh. Unlike Johnny Clem, who earned fame on the Union side as "Johnny Shiloh" or the "Drummer Boy of Chickamauga" because of his courage on the battlefield, the Drummer Boy of Shiloh remains anonymous to this day. Legend has it that on the second day of battle, a drummer boy with Buell's regiments was ordered to sound the drum roll, "Attack." Heeding the drum roll, Union soldiers advanced toward the Confederate positions near Shiloh Church. As resistance from the Confederates intensified, a Union officer yelled to the drummer boy to sound the drum roll for "Retreat." Instead of doing as he was ordered, the drummer boy played the drum roll for "Attack." The officer ran up to the drummer boy and demanded to know why he had not obeyed his command. "'Attack' is all I know," the drummer boy replied. To the officer's surprise, however, his soldiers charged uphill in the face of the withering fire from above and drove the Confederates back. After the smoke had cleared, the commander searched for the drummer boy who had saved the day. He was found lying dead on the hillside, still clutching his drumsticks.

For years, most historians believed the story to be nothing more than a romantic folk tale. However, in 1940, a construction crew was creating a new road through the park when they uncovered the skeleton of a child. Pieces of the drum cord were still tied around his neck, and a bullet was lodged in his heart. To this day, visitors to the park still claim to hear the soft drumming of the phantom drummer boy, summoning his soldiers to battle.

One of the stories told by rangers at the park makes one wonder if the phantom drum rolls have not reinvigorated at least one of the fighting spirits at Shiloh. Several years ago, a man was wandering the park at night, searching for relics with a metal detector. The rangers had found evidence that the man had been digging in the park, but they had been unable to catch him in the act. One night, rangers patrolling the park discovered a broken metal detector. Suspecting that the thief was nearby, they began searching the park. Before long, they discovered a car parked by the edge of the woods. Sitting inside the car was the man they had been looking for. They were unable to question him, however, because he was in a state of shock. Later, he was taken to a local hospital for psychiatric care. When the man recovered, he refused to tell authorities what had happened to him that night in the park. Apparently, the spirits of the Shiloh Battlefield do not care how much history visitors absorb during their stay at the park, but they really prefer that all artifacts remain behind.

Shiloh National Military Park is on State Route 22 in Shiloh, Tennessee, twenty-five miles northeast of Corinth, Mississippi.

Loretta Lynn's Ranch

*L*oretta Lynn's thirty-five-hundred-acre Family Campground has a fascinating history. The story goes that Loretta and her husband, Mooney, were taking a back road in the country in the late 1960s when they discovered an old plantation house near the little town of Hurricane Mills. Loretta instantly fell in love with the old home and decided to buy it. Fortunately for Loretta, the house was for sale, and so was the entire town of Hurricane Mills. Loretta bought the house and the adjoining property in 1966. It turned out that the grand antebellum farmhouse was the former home of Colonel James T. Anderson, who built it in 1845. He made his living growing peanuts on his farm. Before the Civil War, the property featured a blacksmith shop, a general store, a stave mill, a woolen mill, a flour mill, a county school, an iron truss bridge over Hurricane Creek, and a Church of Christ meetinghouse. Hurricane Mills was one of the first towns in Tennessee to generate electricity. The town's generator was housed in Anderson's gristmill. Today, the surviving buildings form the nucleus

242

of Loretta Lynn's Western Town. Testimony from visitors suggests that the past persists in more ways at Loretta Lynn's Family Campground than through the existence of old buildings.

Loretta Lynn realized that there was something different about her house soon after moving in. Several times when Loretta was alone in her bedroom, she saw the door to the adjacent bedroom where her twin daughters slept open and close by itself. Her daughters, Patsy and Peggy, reported seeing the ghostly figures of women dressed in Victorian-era clothing walking around their room. At the time, they were too young to realize that the women were not living beings. Loretta took her children's concerns even more seriously when she began having strange encounters of her own. Several times when Loretta was alone in the house, she felt as if a cold figure had passed right through her body. She also heard the sound of someone walking up the stairs. The scariest place in her house turned out to be the "slave pit," a small dark cellar with iron bars over the top. One evening in 1983, Loretta and a friend named Sue were watching television in the front parlor when they heard the sound of what they thought was someone walking across the front porch. After turning on the porch light and finding nothing, they returned to watching television. Then a few minutes later, they heard someone dragging a chain. They became even more uneasy when they realized that the sound was coming from the slave pit.

Another eyewitness to paranormal activity at Loretta Lynn's Family Campground is a Civil War reenactor named Ken Sumner, who was the Civil War reenactment coordinator for the ranch. Sumner has conducted three reenactments there, the last one in 2001. During one of his visits to the campground, Sumner had a personal encounter with Colonel Anderson's ghost at Loretta Lynn's house: "I had the ghost of the man who had built her house walk up to me, Colonel James T. Anderson. A year later, one of my men told me that he saw him walk down from the house to where I was standing. I was looking in that direction, and no one came down from the house. So we both saw the same apparition that no one else around us had seen. I found out later that Colonel Anderson's ghost has been sighted in the house for years. People have seen the ghost of a slave and a riverboat captain there too." Sumner was also witness to a different type of ghostly activity in the house on another visit to Loretta Lynn's Ranch: "There is the ghost of a little girl in the house, too. We saw the curtain in the house being moved back as if someone was looking out of the windows at us on another separate camp. I was told there was no air-conditioning unit in the second floor that would cause an air current in the house, and the window was shut. That part of the house is closed off. The lower part of the house is used for tour groups."

The ranch's Civil War history might be responsible for the ghosts who have been seen outside the house.

A stockade was built on Colonel Anderson's property. Later on in the war, it was captured and burned. Nineteen Confederate soldiers were killed in a skirmish fought on the property, and their bodies were buried on the grounds. One afternoon, Sumner came face-to-face with the spirits of one of these men: "A man dressed in a Confederate uniform walked up to me and stood across the fire from me. When I looked back at him, I thought he was one of my reenactors. When I started to speak to him, he vanished, and where he vanished, the last I saw of him was his feet vanish and the leaves blowing away from where he was standing. The only problem was, that afternoon they had just cut the grass. The grass wasn't over half an inch high. It was like a carpet. There were no leaves whatsoever on the green. I walked back to camp and told my men what had happened."

During a "Living History Demonstration," Sumner's recreation of life in a Confederate camp turned out to be much more realistic than he had expected it to be: "I had a Confederate soldier standing behind me in Loretta Lynn's front yard during one of our living-history demonstrations when all my troops were down across the creek in Western Town. They saw him standing with me in broad daylight. I caught a glimpse of him out of the corner of my eye, thinking he was one of my people. And then later I found out there had been nobody there."

In the early twentieth century, the Anderson Farm was one of the most progressive farms in the county. Today, it derives its fame primarily from its connection with Loretta Lynn. However, thanks to visitors like Ken Sumner, the site is beginning to acquire a reputation as a very haunted place. Sumner would like to return to the campground, despite the fact that he has had what he describes as "some very startling experiences there."

Loretta Lynn's Ranch and Family Campground is in Hurricane Mills, sixty-five miles west of Nashville. Travel on Interstate 40 to Exit 143. The phone number is 931-296-7700.

Hoskins Library, University of Tennessee

KNOXVILLE

*T*he University of Tennessee in Knoxville is, without a doubt, one of the most haunted campuses in the entire state. For example, a women's dormitory named Strong Hall is haunted by the ghost of Sophronia Strong, whose house once sat on the site of the residence hall. Another dormitory, Reese Hall, is said to be haunted by the spirits of the Native

246

Americans buried beneath the building. Students walking around "the Hill" often hear gunfire still echoing from the Battle of Fort Sanders. Some students have even crossed paths with a spectral wolf in this vicinity. Tyson Hall, a renovated home where the Lutheran Campus Ministries is located, is haunted by a dog, Benita, whose barking can still be heard. However, the ghost that haunts the Hoskins Library announces its presence in a far different way.

The Hoskins Library was actually built in three stages. The first portion of the Hoskins Building was constructed in 1931 as a replacement for the Carnegie Library that had been built on campus around the turn of the century. In 1959, after open stacks had become fashionable, the old stack wing was pulled down, and a new one was built in its place. In 1960, the Special Collections Department opened its doors in the new section. One final addition to the library, the Estes Kefaufer Wing, was constructed in 1966. It is used primarily for meetings and exhibits.

For over twenty years, some librarians have had some weird experiences in the Hoskins Library. Several years ago, the director's secretary received a very strange report from one of the cleaning women. She and her coworkers were waxing the floors when she saw a shadow pass across a doorway leading to the basement. She was so unnerved by the sighting that she had to sit down and catch her breath. The most commonly told story about the library concerns strange food smells. Nick Wyman, the director of the Rare Books and Manuscripts Division, says that on several occasions, he has gone down to the stacks in the basement and smelled something like a casserole cooking. Wyman found the smells to be particularly unsettling because "this was not a place where you could cook food."

An explanation for the unusual occurrences in the building was provided by one of Wyman's coworkers: "She always referred to this phenomenon as the Primrose People. There was a story in *Reader's Digest* entitled 'The Primrose People,' and it was about these people who inhabit populated places. You can't see them, but you know they're there. They appeared in the evening, but you couldn't see them. And the smell of something cooking was linked to the Primrose People in her story. Whenever she smelled food cooking in the stacks, she always said, 'That's the Primrose People cooking.'"

Since the death of his coworker, no one besides Wyman has had contact with "the Primrose People" in the Hoskins Library. Some might argue that the cooking smells emanate from a hungry person's overactive imagination, not from the spirit world. On the other hand, the Hoskins Library could be one of a number of college libraries in the South that have become the earthly home of unearthly residents. To this writer's knowledge, it is the only college library in the United States haunted by "the little people."

The Hoskins Library is on the campus of the University of Tennessee in Knoxville; phone: 865-974-4351.

Walking Horse Hotel

WARTRACE

artrace, Tennessee, derives its name from a trail used by Native Americans. A local legend has it that Andrew Jackson carved "This is Wartrace Creek" into a beech tree near the stream that bears the name today. Wartrace was established as a town in 1851, but it acquired the name "Wartrace Depot" in 1852 after the Nashville and Chattanooga Railroad was completed through eastern Bedford County. At this time, Wartrace was classified as a "tank town" because of its prominent water tank located close to the train tracks. Wartrace eventually became a health resort because of the curative powers of its sulfur springs and wells. Wartrace has had at least six historic inns and hotels since its founding in the 1850s, including the Chockley Tavern, a stagecoach stop that served as the headquarters for Major General Patrick R. Cleburne during the Confederate withdrawal from Murfreesboro in 1862. One of the best known of these old inns is the Walking Horse Hotel, which was added to the National Register of Historic Places in 1984. Originally known as Hotel Overall, the hotel was renamed after the famous Tennessee Walking Horse breed developed by area horsemen in the 1920s and 1930s. In fact, the first grand champion Walking Horse, Strolling Jim, is buried behind the Walking Horse Hotel. George Wright, who managed the Walking Horse Hotel, believes the old inn was haunted by what he terms a "protective spirit."

Although George Wright was manager at the Wartrace Hotel only from 1981 to 1983, he had enough strange experiences there to convince him that something was staying there besides the paying guests. However, he believes that the ghost at the Wartrace Hotel was a benevolent presence that took care of the place: "I can remember several times waking up in the middle of the night and feeling like something was wrong. I'd go downstairs, and the sump pumps would be off, and there'd be two or three inches of water on the floor." On Christmas morning one year, he was at home sitting at the dining room table when he was filled with a sense of dread. He drove over to the Wartrace Hotel and arrived in barely enough time to prevent a fire from starting. He attributes the fact that nothing was ever stolen from the hotel while he was there to the inn's protective spirit.

Wright received tangible proof that his hotel was haunted when he was in the process of making a travel brochure. "I hired a photographer from Massachusetts to come down and shoot some pictures for me," Wright said. "We were shooting some pictures in the dining room, and when he developed them, they had these high-energy lines in them. When he got them back, he called me up and said, 'You're not going to believe this, but . . .' I interrupted him and said, 'Yeah, I'll believe it.'"

Guests also reported seeing something odd in the hotel. "People would come stay at the hotel," Wright said, "and tell me the next morning that they had seen a white apparition on the stairway or at the end of the hall. Some people described it as a moving shadow. None of the guests were ever terrified, though. It was more of a Casper-type ghost, more of a guardian."

Wright was never able to identify the spirit that hovered over his hotel. The ghost could be the spirit of one of the longtime guests who called the hotel home. It could also be the spirit of one of the soldiers who stayed here in the ten-year period that it served as a halfway house for injured veterans. Wright suspects, though, that the haunting of the Wartrace Hotel might be connected somehow to the Waters, who owned the hotel before he did: "Mr. Waters was a big horse trainer here. He bought the hotel in 1939 and operated it until he died in 1942. His wife ran it by herself until 1955. After she died in 1981, the ghost left, too."

Because the haunting activity began soon after Waters died in 1942 and ceased after his wife died in 1981, there is a strong possibility that the ghost of the Wartrace Hotel was the spirit of the former owner. Although George Wright was somewhat relieved when the Wartrace became a "normal" hotel, he was also filled with a sense of regret: "He always looked after me to make sure that I didn't miss out on something bad that was going on at the hotel. It was kind of a treat having him there."

Wartrace is in south-central Tennessee between Shelby-ville and Manchester on Highway 64. The hotel is on Main Street. The mailing address is The Walking Horse Hotel, P.O. Box 266, Wartrace, TN 37183; phone: 423-389-6407.

Texas

Woman Hollering Creek

A map of Guadalupe County indicates that Woman Hollering Creek originates around Marion and flows south toward New Berlin. Most of the year, it resembles more of a trickle than a creek. In fact, Woman Hollering Creek would not merit inclusion in a book of ghost stories were it not for its name. Woman Hollering Creek is a loose translation of La Llorona, which means "weeping woman" in Spanish. According to folklorists, La Llorona exists only in the stories passed down for generations in Mexico. However, many people who live in the area between San Antonio and Seguin have good reason to believe that La Llorona is real.

Stories of La Llorona are very common in west Texas, but they can also be found in New Mexico and Mexico. Although these legends are told primarily within the Hispanic community, many Anglos have also contributed to this growing tradition of ghost narratives. Scholars disagree as to the origin of these legends. Some folklorists say that the origins of the Wailing Woman can be traced back to the Aztecs, who told of a goddess who stole babies from their cradles and roamed around villages shrieking and screaming. Other scholars, though, claim that La Llorona was a prominent figure in Spanish mythology long before the conquistadors made contact with the Aztec. They say that Spanish peasants began telling these stories as far back as the Middle Ages. Regardless of where the stories came from originally, the story of the sorrowful mother is more than just an old tale for thousands of people living in west Texas.

The stories of La Llorona vary in the details, but the core of the story is always the same. Dino Rogelio Quijada, a native of Panama, tells the tale as it was passed down to him by his Spanish ancestors: "People have told this story for generations. I remember when I was a kid, they told this story. La Llorona was a wild woman. A long, long time ago, this woman fell in love with a married man and had a kid. They lived together in a special house that he made for her. When she got pregnant, he told her that he did not want to leave his wife and marry her. She was very sad when she heard this, so after the baby was born she threw him in the river. God put the blame on her for her sin, so he cursed her. Even now, she has to walk every night by the rivers and creeks looking for her baby. People in Panama say that you have to baptize your children because if the child is not baptized, La Llorona will hear the child crying and take it."

In a version provided by Mexican immigrant Jose Guzman, La Llorona's motivation is clouded in mystery: "My father told me one time. This is the first story I listened to [as a child]. It is about a woman who was in love with a man she was not married to. She had three kids. One she gave to the pigs. And one she threw in the river. And one she left alone in the field. Now God put something on [cursed] the woman because it's not right to do that to your kids. Now she has to find the bodies of her children. That's why she has to go from generation to generation [looking for her kids]. So many different people can tell you tales about La Llorona, and so many people can tell you a lot of different tales about her."

Not only do people in west Texas tell the traditional tales about La Llorona, but some of them speak of personal encounters with this ghastly spirit. According to Jose Guzman, his uncle had a terrifying experience with La Llorona: "I had an uncle who said he saw that woman. In the old days, he had a lot of women, and he used to visit them at night. One of his girlfriends lived way out in the country, and he had to walk through rough country to see her. Late one evening, he was walking by a creek, and he saw this beautiful woman. He said to himself, 'What a beautiful woman!' He wanted to talk to her, but he could never get close to her. She kept walking in front of him. When he finally got closer to her, he noticed that she was not stepping on the ground. She was floating over it. He saw her beautiful white dress and long hair, and he wanted her to turn around and show her face. He told her his name and said, 'Turn around. I'd like to meet you.' She asked him three times, 'You are not afraid?' He said, 'I am not afraid,' She said, 'You're sure you're not afraid?' and he said, 'I'm not afraid. I'm a strong man!' She said, 'Well, here I am.' She turned around, and she had no meat on her face. She only had bone. My uncle said the hair stood up on the back of his neck. He said he was very afraid at the moment. He was shaking. He told me, 'I never want to see that woman again!' "

Guzman says the mother of a friend of his had an even more traumatic experience with a beautiful woman in a white dress: "I used to go to her house to see my friend. On two nights, a woman in a white dress walked into her kitchen. [His mother] told him, 'I can't explain it to you, but I saw her. She had long hair and a white dress.' Two months later, she passed away."

In recent years, more first-person testimonies of La Llorona's existence have surfaced. On a wintry day in 1978, Shirley Mackie was walking along Hog Creek near Lake Waco, taking photographs of the snowy landscape. When she developed the film, Mackie was shocked to see the image of a woman standing on a promontory less than fifty feet from the camera. The woman clearly had a seductive figure and the face of an animal. She was holding a baby. Mackie swears that the image was not visible with the naked eye. After the

Waco *Tribune* ran a copy of the photograph, Mackie received a visit from fifty-year-old Lorenzo Gayton, who said that the image in the photograph was the same woman he saw along Hog Creek as a boy.

Most of the Hispanic people who tell the story of La Llorona are fully aware of its subtexts. To girls, the story is a warning against the seductive power of men. To mothers, the story exhorts them to place the love of their children above everything else. To men, the sad tale presents the far-reaching consequences of exploiting women for a few nights' pleasure. To children, La Llorona is a phantom who will "get" them if they wander too close to the water. For most of the rest of us, La Llorona is a myth, a denizen of our nightmares. However, the stories told by eyewitnesses suggest that La Llorona might be much more than just a fairy tale.

Woman Hollering Creek is off Interstate 10 between Santonio and Seguin, just before the FM 755 exit to New Berlin.

DeWitt County Courthouse

Named after colonizer Green DeWitt, DeWitt County was created from parts of Gonzales, Victoria, and Goliad counties. Since the county's inception, there have been three courthouses in three different cities. On April 8, 1894, the second courthouse was torched. The arsonist might have been a lover of beauty because the April 12, 1894, edition of the *Hallettsville Herald* said the courthouse had been an eyesore for many years. The architect who was hired to build the new courthouse, A. O. Watson, had difficulty securing funding for the project. His financial problems became so severe that in December 1896, workers who had not been paid in weeks walked off the job before the roof was completed. After Watson went broke, he was replaced by Eugene Heiner. Construction of the Romanesque Revival structure was completed in 1897. It is built of sandstone and pink granite quarried from Marble Falls, but its most distinctive features were the lighted clock on the north side of the building and the four finials that topped the corner roofs. Equally famous is the legend of the Lady in the Courthouse Clock.

According to Peggy Ledbetter, the DeWitt County treasurer, the Lady in the Courthouse Clock might have been nothing more than an optical illusion created by the building's unique architecture: "Before we remodeled the courthouse in '57, we had some finials on top. We think that's what was doing it. On a bright, moonlit night, people would drive down here to watch. It looked like a lady going across the face of the clock—a shadow. I have one of the finials in my office that's on loan from a gentleman who has antiques. It [the finial] does go in the middle and out at the bottom like a skirt. They assume that this is what it [the Lady] was, because after the courthouse was remodeled, we didn't see the Lady. I don't know how many years she was seen."

Ledbetter believes that the legend was popularized during World War II by servicemen who had ulterior motives in telling it: "During World War II, we had an airfield here—Brayton Field—and I've had some gentlemen come in—retired—they called it 'Witch of the Clock.' They said they'd bring their dates down here, and if you saw the Lady of the Clock, you got a kiss from your girl." Today, the grandchildren of these couples continue to tell the story: "We had students come here for tours, and I've had little ones say, 'Tell me about the Lady of the Clock' because their grandparents had mentioned it to them."

Many people in Cuero, including Peggy Ledbetter, believe that the remodeling of the old courthouse in 1957 did a lot of damage:"Old-timers told me that there was just a big pile of stuff out on the courthouse lawn and people just took what they wanted."The four finials were removed because officials feared that someone might be killed if they fell off, as one of them did in 1927. Ledbetter hopes that a grant the city has applied for will do more than simply restore the old court-house's Victorian luster:"We're trying to get a grant to preserve the courthouse. A lot of people want to put the finials back. We might get the Lady back, too. Who knows?"

Frances Alexander English, a college instructor, memorialized the Lady of the Clock in a poem entitled "In Cuero Town":

A little old lady lives in a clock
Tick–tock, tick–tock
In Cuero-town
Tick–tock!
On each bright night
When the moon is right,
She tiptoes out
And walks about
Tick–tock, tick–tock
They say the old church steeple knows
When and why she comes and goes.

Tick-tock!
He will not tell
Tick-tock!

The DeWitt County Courthouse is located at 397 North Gonzales, Cuero, Texas; phone: 361-275-8897.

The Littlefield Home, University of Texas

AUSTIN

Many universities throughout the Southeast have acquired private homes through expansion and donation. Quite a few of these homes have taken on a second life as office buildings, fraternity or sorority houses, and dormitories. One such structure is the Littlefield Home on the west side of the University of Texas campus. It was built in 1893 at a cost of $50,000 by a cattle baron, banker, and Confederate officer named George Littlefield. Although the Littlefield Home appears to be an anomaly today, in 1893 it was originally nestled in a plush neighborhood populated by other wealthy businessmen, all of whom displayed their wealth by building ostentatious Victorian mansions. In the twenty-first century, the Littlefield Home is the sole remnant of that gaudy era in this section of Austin, its Spanish Renaissance ornamentation a beautiful reminder of a grand period in Austin's history. Today, the second floor of the Littlefield Home houses the offices of the Resource Development Special Programs staff; the first floor is totally unoccupied. For years, students and staff members have shared stories about Major Littlefield's wife, Alice, the melancholy ghost of the Littlefield home.

George Washington Littlefield was born in Mississippi in 1842. He and his family moved to Gonzales, Texas, in 1850. In 1861, Littlefield enlisted as a private in Terry's Texas Rangers. He saw action at Shiloh, Murfreesboro, and Chickamauga and rose to the rank of captain. In 1862, while on a trip to Texas to enlist new recruits, Littlefield also found the woman he was to marry. Early in 1863, he and Alice Payne Tiller married. On December 26, 1863, Littlefield was severely wounded at Mossy Creek in eastern Tennessee. Left for dead on the battlefield, Littlefield managed somehow to return to Texas, lame and on crutches. By 1867, he was walking well enough to take control of the family's plantation. After planting—and losing—three consecutive crops in 1868, 1869, and 1870, he decided to go into the cattle business. In 1871, Littlefield collected his cattle, bought other stock on credit, and drove his herd north to the Kansas cattle markets in 1871. A few months later, he returned to Texas with enough money to pay off his debts. For the next thirteen years, Littlefield set about building a ranching empire in west Texas.

In 1883, Major Littlefield, as he was now known, moved his home and operations to Austin. He also found time to organize the American National Bank in 1890. By 1893, he was ready to build the type of palatial home suitable for a man of his wealth and station. San Antonio architect James W. Wahrenberger envisioned a luxurious mansion that resembled a Victorian fairyland castle. He added such fanciful flourishes as dormers, spires, turrets, mansards, cornices, and finials that seemed to sprout from the red fish-scale slate-tile roof. The foundation and sills were made from sandstone quarried from Pecos, Texas. The bricks were "imported" from St. Louis, Missouri, at a cost of ten cents each. Littlefield was so proud of his new home that he had his initials, "GWL," chiseled in the limestone capitals that top the columns flanking the front door. Other sets of his initials are scattered throughout the home. Final costs for the construction of the Littlefield Home totaled $50,000, a princely sum in 1893.

After Littlefield died in 1920, Alice Littlefield continued living in the house until her death in 1935, when the house was given to the University of Texas. In 1936, the staff members of the local State of Texas Centennial Exposition moved into the home. They stayed until the celebration was over. In 1938, the UT-Austin music department moved into the house and resided there until 1942. The Naval ROTC resided there from 1942 to 1957. In 1957, the house was repaired and repainted. For the next ten years, the students from the music department practiced in little cubicles in the basement. Then in 1967, the Littlefiled Home was completely renovated with $90,000 donated by the Friends of the University. Today, the University Development Board office is on the second floor. The first floor is open to visitors Monday through Friday, 8 A.M. to 5 A.M.

The Victorian and Gothic elements of the Littlefield House suggest that ghosts might be lurking inside. Testimony provided by the people who have worked here over the years confirms that initial impression. In recent years, staff members have sensed that they are not alone in the old house. In fact, most of them do not look forward to being the first ones in the building or the last to leave. Ruth Stone, the senior event planner, said that after returning from vacation one cold, wintry day, she and her coworkers found two candelabra from the fireplace mantle lying on the floor, several feet from the fireplace. The house had been completely empty during break. Stone also said that when her four-year-old granddaughter entered the Littlefield House for a visit, her first words were, "Someone dead is here." A similar sentiment was expressed by event planner Carol Sablan's young son, who told her that he felt "creeped out" in the house. During one visit, he complained, "I really, really don't like it here."

As in many old houses, the "spookiest" area in the Littlefield Home is the attic. In this case, the attic's ghostly aura has as much to do with local legend as it does with dark shadows and filmy spider webs. Supposedly, shortly after the Civil War, Major Littlefield locked his wife, Alice, in the attic while he was away for fear that she might be attacked by Yankees seeking revenge. Alice's confinement only aggravated the mental illness that plagued her in later years. According to one account, Alice was assaulted by bats during her confinement, and some people claim that her shrieks can still be heard coming from the attic. Others say that her ghost has been seen peering anxiously out of the attic windows, waiting for her husband's return. Interestingly enough, a small round window in one of the attic turrets is occasionally shuttered, despite the fact that the window is accessible only by climbing into the attic and crawling through a small hole to the interior of the turret.

Is the house's ghostly mystique a product of the dim illumination and dark wooden shutters? Does Alice Littlefield's brooding presence still haunt the Littlefield House? University officials would prefer that the Littlefield House be viewed as a monument to a wealthy man's generous contributions to the campus of the University of Texas. One cannot deny, however, that Major Littlefield's legacy also includes the ghost stories that have become an important part of campus lore.

The Littlefield House stands on the corner of Twenty-fourth Street and Whitis Avenue on the west side of the University of Texas at Austin campus.

Excelsior House Hotel

JEFFERSON

*T*he Excelsior House Hotel in Jefferson has gained notoriety for several reasons. Built in the 1850s, it is the oldest continuously operated hotel in Texas. The Excelsior has also gained fame as the place where some of the most famous celebrities of the nineteenth century stayed. In the original registers in a glass case in the lobby, one can see the signatures of millionaire John Jacob Astor and Presidents Rutherford B. Hayes and U. S. Grant. British poet and playwright Oscar Wilde, stayed at the hotel on March 31, 1882, and again on April 5, 1882. In the twentieth century, Lady Bird Johnson visited the Excelsior. The most famous signature is that of multimillionaire railroad tycoon Jay Gould, who signed with the likeness of a jaybird for his first name. For over thirty years, though, the Excelsior Hotel has achieved the status of being one of the most haunted hotels in the state.

According to the cleaning women and a few visitors, at least three of the rooms in the old section of the Excelsior are haunted. Over the years, people have heard strange noises at night in the rooms where President U. S. Grant stayed in 1883 and where Rutherford B. Hayes stayed in 1878. In 1970, a woman sleeping in the Rutherford B. Hayes Room claimed that unseen hands kept pulling the covers off her in the four-poster bed. The next morning, she told the staff that her door had been locked the entire night.

The most haunted room in the entire hotel is undoubtedly the Jay Gould Room. When Gould stayed there in the 1870s, he left without paying his bill. The reason can possibly be found in the register, where, below his name, he predicted the "end of Jefferson" because the town would not cooperate with him on the construction of his railroad. Some of the staff at the Excelsior are not convinced that Gould has really left. Senior cleaning woman Ruby Britton has sensed a presence in the room during rainstorms. Even more terrifying was the headless apparition that greeted her as she entered the Jay Gould Room one day. After that encounter, Ruby refused to go into the Jay Gould Room unless accompanied by another person.

Famed film director Steven Spielberg claimed to have had a very weird experience in the Jay Gould Room as well. He spent the night there in 1974: "The old hotel in Jefferson, Texas, really freaked me out. We pulled in there one night and dragged ourselves upstairs after a rough day of filming *Sugarland Express*. I swear my room was haunted. I made everyone pack up and leave at two o'clock in the morning. We drove to the nearest Holiday Inn and everyone was hot at me. Normally, I'm not superstitious."

In the 1970s, newspaper columnist Frank X. Tolbert decided to test the validity of these stories by spending several nights in the Jay Gould Room. Once, when Tolbert stayed in the room by himself, he was awakened at 3:35 A.M. by the siren from a nearby fire station: "I switched on a light and the first thing I noticed was that the wardrobe doors were open. I closed the doors firmly and went back to bed. When I awoke about 6 A.M., the wardrobe doors were open again." A quick check of the doors revealed that they had secure latches. Apparently, the unseen visitor in the room also played with the bedroom door: "The door into the big bathroom slammed shut a couple of times, although there was no breeze in the room." When Tolbert and his family stayed there in February 1976, his son mentioned that several times during the night, he had heard a man and a woman conversing in cultured accents in the attic. Cissie McCampbell, the manager of the Excelsior, told Tolbert that if a man and woman were occupying the attic during the night, they certainly were not paying guests.

Many of the guests at the Excelsior House Hotel are lured there by the luxurious nineteenth-century

splendor of the rosewood, cherry, and mahogany furnishings. Others are attracted by the prospect of sleeping
in one of the historic bedrooms. Then there are those
people like Frank Tolbert, who visit the old hotel in the
hope of discovering for themselves if the old stories are
really true.

The Excelsior House Hotel is located at 211 West
Austin, Jefferson, Texas; phone: 903-665-2513.

Virginia

Bunnyman Bridge

olklorist Jan Harold Brunvand defines urban legends as "legends that—unlike myths—are set in the recent past and involve normal human beings rather than ancient gods or demigods." The most enduring urban legends are those reflecting the fears and anxieties of our time. The "vanishing hitchhiker" legends, for example, have been exploiting drivers' fears of picking up strangers for over a century. Many of the scariest urban legends have been created by teenagers who have rejected the far-fetched plots of fairy tales in favor of more plausible stories with realistic settings. The characters in these stories are much like the young people who tell them: babysitters, necking couples, and students. In many of these tales, the hapless protagonists find themselves caught up in threatening circumstances. One of the strangest of these grisly tales is the legend of Bunnyman Bridge.

Like most legends, the story of Bunnyman Bridge has several variants. The most commonly told—and historically accurate—version is set in Fairfax County, Virginia. In 1905, local residents forced the closure of a state mental hospital. During transit to a nearby hospital, two patients, Marcus Walster and Douglas Griffin, escaped and hid out around an old bridge. A few days later, Walster was found hanging by a noose from a tree. As a result of a number of rabbit carcasses found near the bridge, the remaining fugitive was called "the Bunnyman" by locals. Some people say he ate the rabbits, while others claim that he fashioned clothing out of their skins. Locals also disagree about the fate of the Bunnyman. Some say he ran into the path of an oncoming train while being pursued by authorities. Others swear that the Bunnyman escaped into the woods and was never seen again.

In a less popular version of the story, the Bunnyman was a deranged teenage boy. One Easter morning, he woke up, put on an Easter Bunny costume, and murdered his entire family. Covered in blood, he walked over to the bridge and hanged himself. At the time of his death, he was still wearing his bunny costume.

A series of bloody murders at the bridge ensured that the Bunnyman will never be forgotten. Since 1905, twenty-eight deaths have taken place at the bridge. One legend has it that in 1943, two teenage boys were found hanging from one end of the bridge, and a girl was hanging from the other end. All three had been disemboweled. A similar incident occurred in the summer of 1974. A group of six teenagers who had planned to drink beer on the railroad tracks above the bridge one night failed to return home. They were found the next day, gutted and hanging from the bridge.

For almost a century, visiting Bunnyman Bridge in the dead of night has become a rite of passage for teenagers in Fairfax County. Generations of young people have ventured alone to the middle of Bunnyman Bridge and chanted, "Bunnyman! Bunnyman! Bunnyman!" in an effort to call forth his spirit. Although the Bunnyman haunts the bridge every night, he is said to become visible only on Halloween night.

Regardless of whether or not the Bunnyman is real, the Fairfax County Police Department believes that the danger in that remote area is very real. Several years ago, a surveillance camera was installed to catch teenagers getting in trouble. While it is true that the popularity of the legend has caused some young people to be injured at the site, the legend does perform a useful function. The story is still passed down because of its message. Lovers Leaps, abandoned houses, and old bridges might seem to be attractive places to party, far from the prying eyes of parents and police, but the risks involved (e.g., pregnancy, sexually transmitted diseases, and drunk driving accidents) outweigh any thrills one might derive from breaking the rules.

Bunnyman Bridge is in Fairfax Station, Virginia. Take Chapel Road to Colchester Road. Drive all the way down the road until you round a slight corner. Bunnyman Bridge is completely shrouded in viney overgrowth.

Chatham Manor

FREDERICKSBURG

*C*hatham Manor in Fredericksburg, Virginia, has some very strong links to America's colonial past. In 1728, William Fitzhugh built the great Georgian mansion he named Chatham for a classmate of his at Eaton and Oxford—William Pitt, Earl of Chatham. George Washington, a frequent visitor to Chatham, wrote, "I have put my legs oftener under your mahogany at Chatham than anywhere else in the world, and have enjoyed your good dinners, good wine, and good company more than any other" (Lee 1966, 27). Marguerite DuPont Lee, author of *Virginia Ghosts*, explained the allure this magnificent mansion has held for generations of Virginia's aristocracy: "Those were the days of the crinoline and brocade, of knee-breeches and powdered wigs; when casks of Burgundy and Madeira graced the cellar, and mint juleps quenched the thirst at all seasons and at all hours" (27). During the Civil War, the estate served as the Union headquarters for generals such as Irvin McDowell, Rufus King, John Gibbon, Ambrose Burnside, and Edwin Sumner. Another president, Abraham Lincoln, visited the home while inspecting the troops. The house also served as an artillery post, communications hub, and field hospital. Two of the most illustrious nurses of the entire Civil War, Clara Barton and poet Walt Whitman, cared for the injured here. Although Chatham Manor has seen more than its share of death and misery over the years, the ghost legend associated with the old house springs, not from war, but from an ill-fated love affair.

Tour guide Elsa Lohman believes that the ghost story first surfaced in the twentieth century: "The way that I understand it is that this story popped up in the twentieth century from the last homeowner's wife. I can't remember her first name. She started telling the story of a young lady who was well known to the Washington and Fitzhugh families. She was from a wealthy family who visited Europe to become acculturated over there, like upper-class families did back then. She met a young man—a drysalter, I believe—who was beneath her station in life and fell in love with him. Her family didn't like it. They discouraged her, but she pursued him. They finally decided to take her back to the U.S. and try to separate her from this young man who ended up pursuing her across the ocean and finding her here in Chatham, where she was visiting the Fitzhughs. George Washington was here as a guest. He discovered the young man trying to elope with her, and he discouraged him. He told him of the error of his ways. He decided that he would leave his young lady friend to a better life, but that broke her heart, and apparently it eventually killed her from woe over losing him."

In her book *Virginia Ghosts*, Marguerite Dupont Lee reports that the girl eventually married a man of her father's choosing and lived long enough to have ten children. However, she never forgot her first true love. Just before she died on June 21, 1790, she announced her intention of walking in spirit on the anniversary of her death in the Lady's Walk on the terrace at Chatham.

Elsa Lohman says that the young woman's ghost, known as the Lady in White, has been seen many times on the grounds over the years. However, she only shows up every seven years on June 21 between noon and midnight. According to Marguerite Dupont Lee, Mrs. Randolph Howard, who was hostess at Chatham for many years, claimed to have seen the Lady in White in the garden walking up and down a path leading to the terrace below. The last time she was seen at Chatham was 1986. Visitors to Chatham have also seen a spectral carriage with people in it going down the driveway. Unfortunately, no one has been able to identify any of the passengers.

Considering the number of people who died at Chatham during the Civil War, Elsa Lohman is surprised that more ghosts are not walking the halls of Chatham: "Actually, the house is remarkably free of any stories about any apparitions showing up anywhere. Chatham and Fredericksburg have a very low number of stories associated with them, especially during the Civil War era." As far as most people are concerned, though, one ghost in the house is quite enough.

Follow Williams Street south to Chatham Manor, also known as Lacy House. Ghost Walk is the path at Chatham leading to a high bluff overlooking the Rappahannock River. The address for Chatham Manor is 120 Chatham Lane, Fredericksburg, VA 22405; phone: 540-373-4461.

Kenmore Plantation and Gardens

FREDERICKSBURG

Kenmore Manor in Fredericksburg, Virginia, was built in 1752 by Fielding Lewis, an arms manufacturer. Lewis's wife, Betty, was George Washington's only sister. The couple lived at Kenmore for forty-five years. According to local legend, George Washington designed the ceilings and employed two

Hessian soldiers captured at the Battle of Trenton to carry out his plan. In 1775, the Virginia Assembly appointed Colonel Lewis chief commander of a "Manufactory of Small Arms" to be created at Fredericksburg. By 1776, the plant was fully operational, and it continued to supply weapons throughout the Revolutionary War. Unfortunately, the government reneged on its promise to provide financial support, and Lewis lost his private fortune. Finally Kenmore was sold to satisfy his creditors. Some say that the restless spirit that walks the halls of Kenmore is the anxious ghost of Fielding Lewis.

For many years, visitors to Kenmore have seen a man dressed in Revolutionary-period clothing pacing around the house looking worried. People who say they've seen him poring over sheets of paper assume that it's Fielding Lewis worrying about his debts. Some employees have seen ghostly figures that disappear suddenly both outside on the grounds and inside the building. Poltergeist-like activity is also common at Kenmore. There have been reports of objects and furniture being moved. A book or vase might be in one place at night and another place in the morning. Doors stubbornly refuse to open or open by themselves. Some tour guides have heard footsteps in the house when no one else is there.

The house was used as a hospital by Union troops during the Civil War following the Battle of the Wilderness. It is believed that some soldiers died here, but only a few. There are three gravesites on the grounds where soldiers who died here were buried. After the war, they were moved to cemeteries. Evelyn Kealy, a volunteer who worked on the archeological digs at Kenmore, had an encounter with one of these individuals in the basement. It was four o'clock in the afternoon, and she was taking a bucket of water outside to empty it when her attention was directed to the darkest part of the basement. Standing against the wall was a tall figure wearing a cape and some sort of military uniform. Evelyn could make out his head, shoulders, and upper torso, but the figure did not seem to have any legs. For a few seconds, she stood there, transfixed. Finally, she walked outside and poured out the water. When she returned, the strange visitor was gone. Later, after she had had time to think about what she had just seen, Evelyn surmised that he could have been a wounded soldier who had had his legs amputated at Kenmore.

In 1971, just five days before Halloween, a séance was conducted at Kenmore by a woman named Grace Walker, a member of the International General Assembly of Spiritualists. A number of people were present, including Colonel Robert Burhans, then-director of Kenmore. As Mrs. Walker walked through the children's room, she said she felt "utter confusion and sadness." She and her guests moved to the master bedroom where the doors had opened and shut by themselves on occasion. The members of the group sat in a circle while Mrs. Walker attempted to make contact with the spirits of Kenmore. She said she saw an older man, "tired and weary of life," dressed in post-Revolutionary War attire. Mrs. Walker also felt the presence of a much younger man who she said was responsible for the swinging doors. He was doing this, she said, as a prank.

Down through the years, other "weird things" have occurred at Kenmore. One night, a security guard was eating a sandwich in the gift shop in the basement when he noticed the doorknob beginning to turn very slowly. When he opened the door, there was no one there. On another occasion, the same security guard saw a lady wearing a veil standing by the gate. She crossed the brick walkway, and when she reached the other side, she vanished. Evelyn Kealey said that occasionally the lights go off by themselves in the basement. On several occasions, Evelyn left the basement door open and returned to find it locked.

In recent years, the ghostly activity at Kenmore appears to have subsided. The only ghost stories one hears anymore are the ones told by former employees. If the ghosts have indeed abandoned the old house, one can only hope that they have found rest, especially Fielding Lewis, the melancholy spirit of Kenmore.

The Kenmore Plantation is located at 1201 Washington Avenue in Fredericksburg, Virginia; phone: 540-373-3381.

Bacon's Castle

Bacon's Castle in Surry, Virginia, is not only one of the oldest brick houses in the United States, but it is also a rare example of Jacobean architecture in America. It was built in 1665 by a prosperous planter named Arthur Allen. By 1652, when he was appointed one of the justices of the peace for Surry County, he had become one of the wealthiest men in the county. In 1665, he built Bacon's Castle on five hundred acres of land he had bought four years earlier from John and Peleg Dunstan. After Arthur Allen died on March 10, 1669, his mansion was passed down to his son, Arthur Allen II. In 1676, Arthur, who was usually known as Major Allen, sided with Governor Berkeley during Bacon's Rebellion. In September of that year, Major Allen left his estate to help Berkeley attack the rebels from a ship in the York River. In Allen's absence, Nathaniel Bacon and his followers occupied and garrisoned Bacon's Castle. Over the next three months, they plundered the house, ate his cattle, ground his wheat into meal, and trampled his crops. After the rebels fled Bacon's Castle the night of December 27, Major Allen sued the rebels for 250 pounds of tobacco each as reparations for the damage they had inflicted on his estate. A number of different people owned Bacon's Castle in the eighteenth century. In 1844, John Henry Hankins bought the old house and later built a Greek Revival addition. In 1889, Charles Warren purchased the house, which remained in the Warren family until the death of his grandson, Walker Pegram Warren, in 1972. Due in large to the Association for the Preservation of Virginia Antiquities, Bacon's Castle was restored and opened to the public in 1983. The legend of the flaming ghost is as much a part of Bacon's Castle as the massive hand-hewn beams and the eighteenth-century furnishings.

According to tour guide Valerie Delgado, Bacon's Castle's signature ghost story explains the origin of a fireball that has been sighted on the grounds many time in the past three centuries: "It's known as Bacon's Castle light or fireball. The light was often seen to enter the house. It would come onto the grounds always on a certain side and enter the west side of the house up in the garret windows. People developed stories about people who died here, and the fireball was a manifestation of their spirit. They tell a story of a young girl who went off in the night to visit a suitor whom her parents didn't approve of. On returning back to her room, she had a candle. If she put a candle in her window, that meant that she would be ready to come out, and so he would know that he was to wait for her on the edge of the property. When she was returning and coming in through the window, she caught her hair alight, and went up in flames before he was able to save her. She tried to leave the house to get him to help her, but it was too late. She was too late. She was engulfed in flames." Locals claim to have seen the strange light for many years following the young woman's death, leading one to speculate that the fireball might actually be the ghostly figure of a young girl in flames running in and around the mansion.

Less spectacular are the stories about poltergeist-like activity in Bacon's Castle: "The last owners told some stories about different articles of furniture," Delgado said. "If a spirit wanted a piece of furniture in a particular spot, and you moved it, the next morning it would be back in the original spot. They heard footsteps on the stairs, footsteps behind you, and a rocking chair that would rock when there was no occupant."

Some say that the ghost of Bacon's Castle sometimes assumes a more conventional form. In the summer of 2001, a tour guide swore that he saw a ghost standing at the end of the driveway. She appeared to be a young girl with brunette hair dressed in a white Victorian-era dress. He said that he saw her walk behind a brick pillar at the end of the driveway, but he never saw her come back through on the other side. Delgado says that a few days later, a young woman told the tour guide that she too saw one of the spirits: "I was up on the porch tower looking down on the garden, I saw a girl walking through the garden. She had on a long white dress and long brown hair." Shocked by what he had just heard, the tour guide replied that her description of the ghost sounded much like the apparition he had seen just a few days before." Delgado says that this was the last time that the ghost has been seen at Bacon's Castle.

Some of the ghost stories that still circulate at Bacon's Castle focus around an old barn in the back yard that blew down years ago. The barn was noteworthy for a cupola that resembled that found on schools or churches. One tour guide who has been working at Bacon's Castle recalled going into the barn one day and hearing the bell ringing. She dismissed the incident as a figment of her imagination until a few weeks later when an elderly gentleman who grew up in the area told her that when he was a boy playing hide and seek in the area, he could hear the bell ringing too. Afterward, the tour guide was relieved to know that she was not losing her mind, but she never felt the same about the old barn.

After working five years in Bacon's Castle, Valerie Delgado has never seen the ghost in any form. In fact, she is convinced that most of the stories people tell about the source of the light are nothing more than local folklore. However, not everyone who has visited the castle agrees that the fireball of Bacon's Castle is just a legend. In 1986, a large group of tourists witnessed the fireball at the same time. Was this sighting the product of mass hysteria, or could it be something else?

Bacon's Castle is near the junction of Highways 10 and 31 in Surry County. The mansion is five miles southeast of Surry, in Smithfield, at the intersection of Highway 10 and County Road 617. The phone number is 757-357-5976.

BIBLIOGRAPHY

Age, Keith. "The Talbott Inn." 1999. http://www.louisvilleghosthunters .homestead.com/Talbott.html.

Ahart, Larry. Personal interview. 31 March 2003.

Albu, Susan H., and Elizabeth Arndt. *Here's Savannah: A Journey through Historic Savannah and Environs.* Savannah, Ga.: Atlantic Printing Company, 1994.

"All about Ghosts." Web site: http://www.allaboutghosts.com.

Babb, Becky. Personal interview. 10 February 2003.

"Bacon's Castle." www.apva.org/apva/bacon.html.

Ball, Bobbie. Personal interview. 7 April 2003.

Beattie, Raejean. Personal interview. 7 May 2003.

Beck, Kevin. Personal interview. 2 April 2003.

Bergeron, Kat. "Gulf Coast Spooks, Old Ones and New, Still Can Produce a Nightmare or Two." *Sun/Daily Herald,* 1 November 1981: C-1, C-6.

Betts, Edward Chambers. *Historic Huntsville.* Birmingham, Ala.: Southern University Press, 1966.

Blitzer, Carol Anne. "Capitol Castle." *Advocate,* 27 March 2000.

Bowerman, Paul. Personal interview. 17 April 2003.

Boyd, Scotty Ray. Personal interview. 2 May 2003.

Bridgewater, Mark. "Old Boston House Haunted by Titillating Ghost Tales." *Palm Beach Post,* 31 October 1992.

"A Brief History of Bacon's Castle." *Jamestown Historic Briefs,* 12 April 1999.

Brown, Alan. *Literary Levees of New Orleans.* Montgomery, Ala.: Black Belt Press, 1998.

———. *Shadows and Cypress: Southern Ghost Stories.* Jackson, Miss.: University Press of Mississippi, 2000.

Brown, Marilyn. Personal interview. 24 July 2002.

Bibliography

Brown, William E., and Karen Hudson. "Henry Flagler and the Model Land Company." *Tequesta: The Journal of the Historical Association of Southern Florida* (1966): 46–78.

Brunvand, Jan Harold. *The Vanishing Hitchhiker: American Urban Legends and Their Meanings*. New York: W.W. Norton & Company, 1981. Quote from p. 3.

Bynum, Hazel. "The Bodley-Bullock House." *Bloom of the Bluegrass*, May 1988: 1.

Campbell, Nanci. "Suspicion of Arson in Cahill Fire." *Daily Herald*, 19 July 1970: A-1, A-2.

"Clermont and White Hall." www.state.ky.us/agencies/paris/i75frames/whthall-body.htm.

Cobb, Al. *Savannah Ghosts*. Savannah, Ga.: Whitaker Street Books, 2001.

Cobun, Pete. "Historic Railroad Depot Here Saw Exciting Times." *Huntsville Times*, 26 July 1970: 4.

Coleman, Christopher. *Strange Tales of the Dark and Bloody Ground*. Nashville, Tenn.: Rutledge Hill Press, 1998.

———. *Ghosts and Haunts of the Civil War*. Nashville, Tenn.: Rutledge Hill Press, 1999.

Cook, Fred. *The Golden Book of the American Revolution*. New York: Golden Press, 1962.

Deblieux, Freddie. Personal interview. 15 April 2003.

DeBolt, Margaret Wayt. *Savannah Spectres and Other Strange Tales*. Norfolk and Virginia Beach, Va.: Donner Company/Publishers, 2000.

Decker, Pamela. Personal interview. 1 May 2002.

Delgado, Valerie. Personal interview. 4 April 2003.

Denning, Hazel M. *True Hauntings: Spirits with a Purpose*. St. Paul, Minn.: Llwellyn Publications, 1996.

"Destrehan Plantation." www.destrehanplantation.org/welcome.htm.

Edwards, Don. "Haunting Holiday Spirit." *Lexington Herald-Leader*, 21 December 2000.

Erstein, Hap, Kevin D. Thompson, Gary Schwan, and Charles Passy. "Palm Beach's Haunted Museum! Channel 12 Anchor Shot! The Tornado on Stage!" *Palm Beach Post TGIF*, 29 October 1999: 32–33.

Fairley, Laura Nan, and James T. Dawson. *Paths to the Past: An Overview History of Lauderdale County, Mississippi*. Meridian, Miss.: Lauderdale County Department of Archives and History, 1988.

Ferris, D. C., editor. *Macon Beacon*. 28 September 1907.

Bibliography

Flato, Charles. *The Golden Book of the Civil War.* New York: Golden Press, 1961.

Foreman, Laura, ed. *Haunted Holidays.* Singapore: Discovery Communications, Inc., 1999.

Fout, Deborah. Personal interview. 19 December 2001.

Galiano, Amanda. "The Old State House Museum." www.littlerock .about.com/.

"Gallop through History: The Hunt-Morgan House." Pamphlet. Blue Grass Trust for Historic Preservation.

Gordon, John Steel. "The Master Builder." *Audacity* (winter 1966): 40–53.

Gordon, Lois. Personal interview. 17 May 2003.

Gotschall, Nichole. Personal interview. 14 April 2001.

Guest Books. 1891 Castle Inn. 2001–2003.

Guzman, Jose. Personal interview. 2 March 2003.

Hallman, Bonnie. Personal interview. 6 March 2003.

Halton, John C. "The Littlefield Home: A Grand and Stately Victorian Mansion." *Austin Homes and Garden* 2:10 (April 1981): 33–38.

Harwell, Edith. Personal interview. 17 March 2002.

Hauck, Dennis William. *Haunted Places: The National Directory.* New York: Penguin Books, 1996.

"Haunted Arkansas: The Old State House." www.prairieghosts.com/ oldstat.html.

"History of Wartrace, Tennessee." www.historicmainstreetinn.com/ wartracehistory.htm.

Hubbard, Sylvia Booth. *Ghosts! Personal Accounts of Modern Mississippi Hauntings.* Brandon, Miss.: QRP Books, 1992.

Hudson, Julie Enders. "Something Spooky on the Second Floor." *News Tribune,* 17 May 1985: 2.

J.M.P. "The Legend of the Lady in Brown." *Chowanoka,* 1914.

Jamiokowski, Tim. "Boston House in FP Is Added to Register of Historic Places." *News Tribune,* 14 April 1985.

Johnson, F. Roy. *Legends, Myths and Folk Tales of the Roanoke-Chowan.* Murfreesboro, NC: Daily News Co., 1962.

Jones, Melanie. "Spirits Take Shining to Library." *Birmingham News,* 31 October 2001: 1-C.

Koon, David. "Who You Gonna Call?" *Arkansas Times,* 1 November 2002. Online Internet, 10 February 2003.

Lambert, Clay. "Treasure Coast Boasts Host of Haunted Houses." *Palm Beach Post*, 25 October 1998: 7.

Latham, Sally. "Boston House: A Stately Monument to History." *News Tribune*, 10 March 1974: 11.

Ledbetter, Peggy. Personal interview. 3 April 2003.

Lee, Marguerite DuPont. *Virginia Ghosts*. Berryville, Va.: Virginia Book Company, 1966.

Lefevre, Edwin. "Flagler and Florida." *Everybody's Magazine* 22 (1910): 168–86.

Levatino, Madeline. *Past Master: The History and Hauntings of Destrehan Plantation*. New Orleans, La.: Dinstuhl Printing and Publishing Co., 1991.

List, Gloria. Personal interview. 25 February 2003.

Lohman, Elsa. Personal interview. 31 March 2003.

Lossing, Benson J. *Our Country*. www.publicbookshelf.com/public_html.

Lucas, Greg. "A Piece of Old Camden Passed Away." *Chronicle-Independent*, 23 November 1984.

Lundahl, Karen. Personal interview. 12 February 2003; 3 March 2003.

Lyon, Ralph. *A History of Livingston University: 1835–1963*. Livingston, Ala.: Livingston Press, 1976.

Mandel, Paul. *Great Battles of the Civil War*. New York: Time, Inc., 1961.

Mauney, Diana. Personal interview. 1 April 2003.

McGonagill, Harriet. "Does Old Stagecoach Inn Have Ghosts?" *Meridian Star*, 30 October 1983: 1-C.

McGonagill, Harriet. Personal interview. 18 December 2001.

McKee, Anne. Personal interview. 1 February 2003.

McKnight, Edgar V., and Oscar Creech. *A History of Chowan College*. Murfreesboro, N.C.: Chowan College, 1964.

McQueen, Keven. *Cassius M. Clay: Freedom's Champion*. Paducah, Ky.: Turner Publishing Company, 2001.

Milstead, Anne. Personal interview. 21 December 2001.

Montgomery, Rachel. "Headless Horseman of Hobkirk Hill." *Camden Chronicle*, 15 November 1970.

"Mordecai Historic Park." www.capitalareapreservation.org/park.html.

Morrero, Ulysses. Personal interview. 20 May 2003.

Mullins, Lashe. Personal interview. 7 April 2003.

Murphy, Donovan. Personal interview. 30 January 2003.

Norman, Michael, and Beth Scott. *Haunted America*. New York: Tom Doherty Associates, Inc., 1994.

Bibliography

Ogden, Tom. *The Complete Idiot's Guide to Ghosts and Hauntings.* Indianapolis, Ind.: Alpha Books, 1999.

"The Old State House." www.aristotle.net.

"Old Statehouse Museum." www.oldstatehouse.com.

Owens, Doug. Personal interview. 25 February 2003.

Perez, Josefina. Personal interview. 2 March 2003.

Phillips, Kendall, and Steve Ziskinder. "The Historic Boston House." *Treasure Coast Times,* October 1999: 9.

"Poem Recalls Courthouse Clock Lady." *Cuero Record,* 27 March 1996.

Preik, Brooks Newton. *Haunted Wilmington and the Cape Fear Coast.* Wilmington, NC: Banks Channel Books, 1995.

Quijada, Dino Rogelio. Personal interview. 2 March 2003.

Randall, Kay. "Littlefield Spirit Lives On: House Is a Victorian Ghost of the Past." www.utexas.edu/features/archive/2002/littlefield.html.

Randolph, Regina. "Margaret Haughery." *Catholic Encyclopedia.* vol. 9. 1910 ed.

Raymond, Robert. "Gray Lady Legend Is One of City's Oldest." *Camden Chronicle,* 15 August 1952.

Reaves, George A., III. "Shiloh." *The Civil War Battlefield Guide.* Ed. Frances H. Kennedy. Boston, Mass.: Houghton Mifflin Company, 1990.

——. "Corinth." *The Civil War Battlefield Guide.* Ed. Frances H. Kennedy. Boston, Mass.: Houghton Mifflin Company, 1990.

Recicar, Jessica. Personal interview. 24 July 2002.

Rhyne, Nancy. *Coastal Ghosts.* Orangeburg, S.C.: Sandlapper Publishing Co., 1985.

Roberts, Nancy. *Georgia Ghosts.* Winston-Salem, NC: John F. Blair, 2001.

Rosta, Katie. Personal interview. 19 March 2003.

Ruiz, Stephanie. Personal interview. 18 May 2003.

Ryan, Pam. "Legend of Spirits Ends with Fire." *Daily Herald,* 19 July 1970: A-1, A-6.

Sargent, Lawrence. Personal interview. 17 May 2003.

"Saving Helen's Bridge." www.asheville.com/news/helen.html.

Schreiber, Peter. Personal interview. 18 May 2003.

Smith, Kalia Katherine. *Journey into Darkness: Ghosts and Vampires of New Orleans.* New Orleans, La.: De Simonin Publications, 1998.

Snider, Neil. Personal interview. 7 February 2003.

Starr, Patti. "Haunted Places in Kentucky." Ghost Chasers International. http://ghosthunter.com and www.pattiacord.com.

Stoltz, Tim. Personal interview. 10 April 2003.

Bibliography

Sumner, Ken. Personal interview. 2 April 2003; 3 April 2003.

Swoops. "DeWitt County Courthouse." www.TexasEscapes.com.

Syers, Ed. *Ghost Stories of Texas.* Waco, Tex.: Texian Press, 1981.

Taylor, Jean. *The Villages of South Dade.* St. Petersburg, Fla.: Byron Kennedy and Company, 1985.

Taylor, L. B.. *The Ghosts of Fredericksburg—and Nearby Environs.* U.S.A.: Progress Printing Co., 1991.

Taylor, Troy. *The Ghost Hunter's Guidebook.* Alton, Ill.: Whitechapel Productions Press, 2001.

———. "Haunted Arkansas: The Old State House." www.prairighosts.com/oldst.html.

———. *Spirits of the Civil War.* Alton, Ill.: Whitechapel Press, 1999.

Tolbert, Frank X. "Night in Jay Gould's 'Haunted' Bedroom." *Dallas Morning News,* 28 February 1972.

———. "A Real Halloween Hotel." *Dallas Morning News,* 31 October 1981.

———. "Spooks in Attic of the Hotel?" *Dallas Morning News,* 14 February 1976.

"Trip to Beautiful Hornibrook Mansion." Web site: www.theempress.com.htm.

Turnage, Sheila. *Haunted Inns of the Southeast.* Winston-Salem, NC: John F. Blair, 2001.

Tyler, Sarah. Personal interview. 10 April 2003.

Warren, Joshua P. *Haunted Asheville.* Asheville, NC: Shadowbox Publications, 1996.

Weaver, Bill. Personal interview. 20 May 2003.

Welch, Jamie. "Who's Haunting Anderson's Corner?" *South Florida History* 26:4 (fall 1998): 25–29.

White, Donna. Personal interview. 26 January 2003.

"White Hall History." www.ket.org/trips/whitehall/history.htm.

Whitmeyer, Cecil. Personal interview. 22 January 2003.

Wiggins, Larry. "The Birth of the City of Miami." *Tequesta: The Journal of the Historical Association of Southern Florida* (1995): 5–38.

Williams, Docia Schultz. *Phantoms of the Plains: Tales of West Texas Ghosts.* Plano, Tex.: Republic of Texas Press, 1996.

Worthen, John M. "The Lady in Black." X-Project Paranormal Magazine. 11 May 2001. Online. 27 January 2003.

Wright, George. Personal interview. 9 April 2003.

Wyman, Nick. Personal interview. 9 April 2003.

INDEX

Index